Bridge With
The Three Musketeers

Bridge With
The Three Musketeers

AKSEL J. NIELSEN

Edited by
DOUGLAS MUNRO

KAYE & WARD
LONDON

First published in Great Britain by
Kaye & Ward Ltd,
21 New Street, London EC2M 4NT
1978

ISBN 0 7182 1201 0

Set in Monotype Baskerville by
Gloucester Typesetting Co. Ltd.
Printed in Great Britain by
Biddles of Guildford

CONTENTS

TO
THE MEMORY OF
MY WIFE

INTRODUCTION

For many years past Aksel J. Nielsen has been adding to his collection of the best Bridge hands that he has come across during his long career as an expert player. Bridge readers wish for more than analyses of various games; they want, in addition, to have instruction and pleasure in their reading and this is what Nielsen has achieved in his new book.

There are few works which have stood the test of time better than Alexandre Dumas' 'The Three Musketeers', originally published in 1844, and Aksel J. has had the idea to transfer around the Bridge table the exploits of Athos, Porthos and Aramis, and the fourth musketeer the brilliant d'Artagnan. In the same adventurous atmosphere as the romance you will be meeting again those four friends playing their cards with the same dexterity as they flashed their swords. The typical traits of each individual character are portrayed as in a living picture.

Until it no longer continued to be published I had, myself, printed several chapters of Nielsen's new book in French in 'Le Bridge'.

When I was asked to write an introduction to his book it was with pleasure that I returned to reading once again and to study, not only the verve and humour, but also the technique and psychology, of 'Bridge With The Three Musketeers'.

José Le Dentu

PROLOGUE

The many admirers of Alexandre Dumas' great romance 'The Three Musketeers' and its sequels will remember that d'Artagnan's servant was Planchet. Later he became an army sergeant, and finally ended up as a well-to-do merchant in Paris. Charles Dickens would have described him as an artful dodger, especially during his service with d'Artagnan; he was that, and a little bit cautious too, but on really serious matters he was, one gathers, trustworthy.

It should be mentioned here that d'Artagnan was a quite outstandingly good bridge player, and that Planchet was trusted sufficiently to kibitz his master's gamesmanship, for which he had a great admiration, and to keep a fairly full record of the various games that were played. When his descendants left France during the Revolution they took with them Planchet's original notes about his master's exploits at the card-table in the company of the three musketeers and others.

If these records had not left France Dumas might very possibly have come across them when he was, with Auguste Maquet, researching archives some two hundred odd years later for further details about the private affairs of the musketeers. For then he would have found characteristics of these men of which he was unaware, but which would emphasise Athos' fairmindedness, the propensity of Aramis to indulge in a little doubtful behaviour now and then, the rather bovine mentality of Porthos, and last, but by no means least d'Artagnan's presence of mind in times of emergency.

It must, of course, be remembered that when d'Artagnan arrived in Paris in 1625 contract bridge as we know it was not then played. But, nevertheless, the game then played, as with most games of skill, gave the clever player opportunities in plenty of beating opponents who were not as bright.

We have tried to transform the card game of the seventeenth century into modern contract bridge so as to give readers, as nearly as possible, the chance of learning about the musketeers' exploits as card-players, exploits until now quite unknown.

* * *

There should first be given a hand which was played when young Charles d'Artagnan, at the age of six, was still at home with his parents at Tarbes. Even at that tender age he was allowed to play when a fourth was needed. Naturally, d'Artagnan must have told Planchet about this hand when he was reminiscing over a bottle of wine.

Dealer: South.
Both vulnerable.

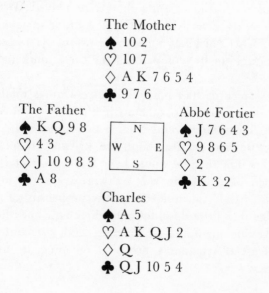

The Mother
♠ 10 2
♡ 10 7
♢ A K 7 6 5 4
♣ 9 7 6

The Father
♠ K Q 9 8
♡ 4 3
♢ J 10 9 8 3
♣ A 8

Abbé Fortier
♠ J 7 6 4 3
♡ 9 8 6 5
♢ 2
♣ K 3 2

Charles
♠ A 5
♡ A K Q J 2
♢ Q
♣ Q J 10 5 4

The bidding 'translated' to bridge:

South	North
1 ♡	2 ◇
3 ♣	3 ◇
4 ♣	5 ♣

D'Artagnan's father led the ♠ K. Charles won with the ace, cashed the ◇ Q and played the ♡ 2 to dummy's ♡ 10 in order to try to get rid of the ♠ 5 on the ◇ A. But Abbé Fortier ruffed with the ♣ 2 and consequently Charles had to overruff. He then tried to get rid of dummy's ♠ 10 by cashing two high hearts, but his father then ruffed with the ♣ 8 which dummy had to overruff. The ◇ K was ruffed by the Abbé with the ♣ 3 which Charles again overruffed, but when he then laid down the ♡ Q he was able to discard dummy's ♠ 10, whether or not his father ruffed with the ♣ A. Had East or West ruffed high earlier then Charles would already have got rid of the spade loser, either from the closed hand or from dummy.

And thus it was that Charles d'Artagnan made a 'Strip-tease Coup' hundreds of years before this 'coup' was re-discovered and received its name.

D'Artagnan also retold the next hand to Planchet from his excellent memory. It was dealt during his stay in an inn in the small town of Vienne when he was on his way to Paris. Unfortunately he could not remember the names of the other players, a curious lapse on his part, but he did remember that he was South.

Dealer: South.
Love all.

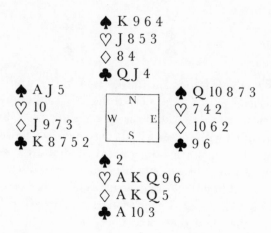

♠ K 9 6 4
♡ J 8 5 3
◇ 8 4
♣ Q J 4

♠ A J 5
♡ 10
◇ J 9 7 3
♣ K 8 7 5 2

♠ Q 10 8 7 3
♡ 7 4 2
◇ 10 6 2
♣ 9 6

♠ 2
♡ A K Q 9 6
◇ A K Q 5
♣ A 10 3

The bidding:

South	West	North	East
2 ♡	Pass	2 NT	Pass
3 ◇	Pass	4 ♡	Pass
6 ♡	Dble.		

It was a stupid double, but West thought that he had two certain tricks, and for safety's sake he took one of them at once laying down the ♠ A and continuing with the ♠ 5.

Without the double d'Artagnan would probably have finessed clubs, but his active and acute brain tried to develop a plan without a finesse—and he found one! First he saw that he could increase his trump tricks to six by ruffing two spades—a method which today we call 'reverse dummy'. He won with dummy's ♠ K, discarding the ♣ 3, and ruffed the ♠ 6 with the ♡ A. The ♡ 9 to the jack over West's ♡ 10 enabled him to ruff dummy's ♠ 9 with the ♡ K, and after having drawn the ♡ Q he cashed the ♣ A! The ♡ 6 was led to dummy's ♡ 8, and on dummy's last trump d'Artagnan discarded the ♣ 10. West was in agony, but seeing the ♣ Q in dummy he had to let go a diamond, whereupon d'Artagnan took the last four tricks in diamonds.

When, at a later date, d'Artagnan told the musketeers about his 'Vienne Coup' Porthos asked him to explain without too much exaggeration the whole idea of it, and Artagnan replied modestly:

'Well, you see, it is a way of squeezing you without squeezing myself!'

PARIS

When he arrived in Paris on his dun-coloured horse and with only fifteen ducats in his pocket d'Artagnan repaired straightaway to call on de Tréville, Captain of the King's Musketeers, at his 'hotel'. There, and to his amazement, he saw three musketeers fighting on a staircase, their swords flashing and cutting, and to him they seemed gods. Clumsily, for he had none of the graces which are taken for granted by those living near the Court, he provoked a duel with one which, in turn, involved duels with the other two.

Duelling was prohibited by Cardinal Richelieu and Athos and d'Artagnan had scarcely drawn swords when a group of the Cardinal's Guard intervened to arrest the three musketeers. The Guards were not interested in d'Artagnan, but he insisted on joining in the resulting fight. The Cardinal's men were routed, with d'Artagnan making a major contribution to their defeat, and from that moment the four victors were firm friends.

Indeed, their victory was celebrated at the inn 'La Truie qui file' over quantities of wine—and bridge. Some of the most interesting hands played that evening follow.

Dealer: South.
Both vulnerable.

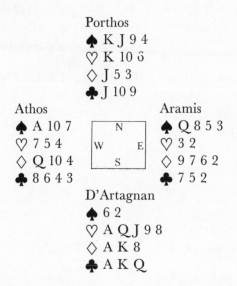

Porthos
♠ K J 9 4
♡ K 10 6
◇ J 5 3
♣ J 10 9

Athos
♠ A 10 7
♡ 7 5 4
◇ Q 10 4
♣ 8 6 4 3

Aramis
♠ Q 8 5 3
♡ 3 2
◇ 9 7 6 2
♣ 7 5 2

D'Artagnan
♠ 6 2
♡ A Q J 9 8
◇ A K 8
♣ A K Q

The bidding:

South	North
2 ♡	2 ♠
2 NT	3 ♡
6 ♡	

Athos led the ♠ 7. D'Artagnan had already found out that Athos was never afraid of running a risk, but he just could not believe that he would lead from the A–Q or even from the queen in Porthos' suit. On the other hand, however, he might very well have underled an ace. If Aramis held both the ace and the queen the contract was doomed at once, but on the principle that two cards can take the jack, but only one the king, d'Artagnan went up with dummy's ♠ K, holding the trick. Then he played the ♡ 6 to the ace and the ♠ 6 from hand, spades being the only suit that would have a small chance of taking care of the diamond loser. Athos won with the ♠ A and shifted to a trump to dummy's ♡ 10.

Why should such a good player as Athos win with the ace? Almost certainly to hide the distribution of the spades—that is, he must hold the lonely ♠ 10 which he would have had to show if not going up with ace. So, d'Artagnan played dummy's ♠ J, ruffed Aramis' queen, played a trump to dummy's king, and discarded the ◊ 8 on the good ♠ 9.

In the next deal a mistake made by Porthos changed into one of luck.

South/Both.

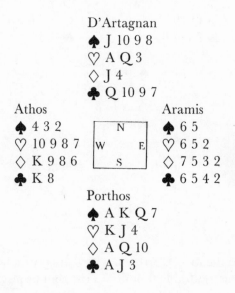

D'Artagnan
♠ J 10 9 8
♡ A Q 3
◊ J 4
♣ Q 10 9 7

Athos
♠ 4 3 2
♡ 10 9 8 7
◊ K 9 8 6
♣ K 8

Aramis
♠ 6 5
♡ 6 5 2
◊ 7 5 3 2
♣ 6 5 4 2

Porthos
♠ A K Q 7
♡ K J 4
◊ A Q 10
♣ A J 3

The bidding: South   North

                  2 ♠   6 ♠

Athos led a trump and Porthos drew two more trumps. Then he led the ♡ 4 to the queen, cashed dummy's ♡ A and led the ♡ 3 to the king, without thinking what he was doing. It was then that he first realised that he might have used dummy's two heart entries to finesse both in clubs and diamonds, which everyone else would have done, and it

would have been sufficient if Aramis held only one of the
kings.

It was, however, too late. There was nothing left for him to
do except to cash the ♣ A and continue with the ♣ J. He
had the colossal good luck that Athos held the ♣ K doubleton
and was endplayed. Whether Athos played a diamond into
the tenace or a heart for a ruff and discard, Porthos needed
only one discard on the clubs.

In the last hand of the evening Aramis did not succeed
with his characteristic duplicity:

South/Both.

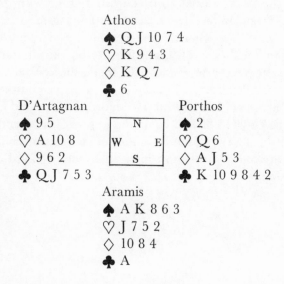

                        Athos
                        ♠ Q J 10 7 4
                        ♡ K 9 4 3
                        ◇ K Q 7
                        ♣ 6

D'Artagnan   Porthos
♠ 9 5   ♠ 2
♡ A 10 8   N   ♡ Q 6
◇ 9 6 2   W   E   ◇ A J 5 3
♣ Q J 7 5 3   S   ♣ K 10 9 8 4 2

                        Aramis
                        ♠ A K 8 6 3
                        ♡ J 7 5 2
                        ◇ 10 8 4
                        ♣ A

The bidding: South   North

                    1 ♠   3 ♠
                    4 ♠

D'Artagnan led the ♣ Q. Aramis won and played the
♠ 3 to the ♠ 10 and the ♠ 4 back to the ace, after which he
played the ◇ 4 to dummy's queen. As Porthos was clever

enough to duck. Aramis took the ♠ J over with the king in order to play the ◇ 8 to the king. It was now that Porthos won with the ace, cashed the ◇ J and shifted to the ♣ K.

Aramis had very little advantage from the ruff with the ♠ 6 and the discard of dummy's ♡ 3. He now led the ♡ 2 and when d'Artagnan followed with the ♡ 8 Aramis fumbled so long with dummy's ♡ 9 that Porthos had his ♡ Q ready. But when Aramis suddenly 'changed his mind' and went up with dummy's king Porthos was so taken by surprise that he inadvertently dropped the queen. Crestfallen he apologised to d'Artagnan, who only laughed.

Now Aramis, who believed and hoped that Porthos also held the ♡ A, wasted no time in continuing with the ♡ 4, but d'Artagnan took two heart tricks and Aramis went down one. Aramis got what he deserved for if he had not been so 'hesitant' with the ♡ 9, making Porthos involuntarily unblock the ♡ Q, he would have made the contract. In the next trick Porthos would have been endplayed on the ♡ Q, and then have had to lead once more to a ruff and discard.

Athos invited his old comrades and his new friend to his rooms in the rue Férou for some rubbers next evening, and here are some of the most interesting hands played on that occasion.

South/Both.

Athos
♠ Q 4 3
♡ 9 8 7
◇ 10 3
♣ A K 7 4 3

Porthos
♠ 6 5 2
♡ A J 6 5 4
◇ K 7 4
♣ 6 2

Aramis
♠ A 10 8 7
♡ Q 2
◇ 9 8 6 5
♣ 10 9 5

D'Artagnan
♠ K J 9
♡ K 10 3
◇ A Q J 2
♣ Q J 8

The bidding:

South	North
1 NT	3 NT

Porthos led the ♡ 5, Aramis played the queen, and d'Artagnan won with the king. He could not see more than seven certain tricks before letting his opponents in, but then he had a sudden shrewd idea. He cashed the ♣ Q and J and shifted to the ♠ K as if he had no more clubs and would try to create an entry with the ♠ Q. But Aramis was far too clever to fall into this trap and let d'Artagnan hold this trick and the next as well on the ♠ J. It was then that d'Artagnan produced his secret weapon—the ♣ 8.

After having cashed the remaining clubs, on which Porthos had to discard a card in each suit, d'Artagnan played dummy's ♡ 9. Porthos could take only three heart tricks, after which he had to play diamonds into the tenace, and a hopeless contract was made with an overtrick.

The echo to show the doubleton club was not then known.

South/Love all.

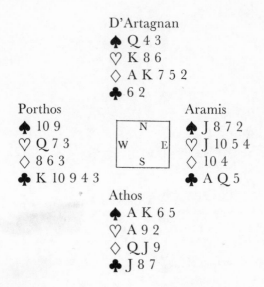

D'Artagnan
♠ Q 4 3
♡ K 8 6
◇ A K 7 5 2
♣ 6 2

Porthos
♠ 10 9
♡ Q 7 3
◇ 8 6 3
♣ K 10 9 4 3

Aramis
♠ J 8 7 2
♡ J 10 5 4
◇ 10 4
♣ A Q 5

Athos
♠ A K 6 5
♡ A 9 2
◇ Q J 9
♣ J 8 7

The bidding:	South	North
	1 ♠	2 ◇
	3 ◇	3 ♠
	4 ♠	

Porthos had the bright idea of opening with the ♠ 10 and was more than a little confused when he was allowed to win the trick. He continued with the ♠ 9, but this time Athos won with dummy's ♠ Q and drew two more rounds of trumps after which he cashed five diamonds and two hearts for ten tricks in all. D'Artagnan congratulated Athos on this beautiful safety play about which Porthos understood nothing, but you, fair reader (as Dumas always wrote), have seen that the contract cannot be made without letting the opponents take the first trump trick.

You must surely have noticed by now that Athos is a gentleman as well as a sportsman. And in the next hand it was by his sportsmanship that he attained a celebrated 'finale.'

North/Both.

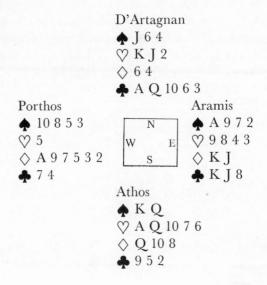

D'Artagnan
♠ J 6 4
♡ K J 2
◇ 6 4
♣ A Q 10 6 3

Porthos
♠ 10 8 5 3
♡ 5
◇ A 9 7 5 3 2
♣ 7 4

Aramis
♠ A 9 7 2
♡ 9 8 4 3
◇ K J
♣ K J 8

Athos
♠ K Q
♡ A Q 10 7 6
◇ Q 10 8
♣ 9 5 2

The bidding:

North	South
Pass	1 ♡
3 ♡	3 NT

The contract could never have been made if Porthos had led a black card, but perfectly naturally he opened with the ◇ 5. Aramis won with the ◇ K and continued with the ◇ J. Although Porthos' rather inferior mental ability is fairly well known it must not be thought that he was a complete idiot at the card table. Certainly he did not understand the finer points of the game, but even so his play was above the average. If this had not been so his friends would have had no pleasure in playing with him. In this case he was well aware that if he won with the ◇ A it would be his last trick. He took the chance of Aramis having the blocking ◇ 10, and ducked.

Athos led the ♣ 9 and let it run, and Aramis, winning with the ♣ J, tried to find a spade entry with Porthos by leading the ♠ 2. Athos won with the king and played the ♣ 5 to dummy's ♣ 10. Aramis won again and once more underled the ♠ A. Athos won with the ♠ Q and now led the ♣ 2 to dummy's queen and then the ♣ 6 on which he discarded the ◇ 10. Following with the ♡ K, the ♡ J, the ♡ 10 and then the ♡ Q Athos won the thirteenth trick which contained *all four aces*!

North/Love all.

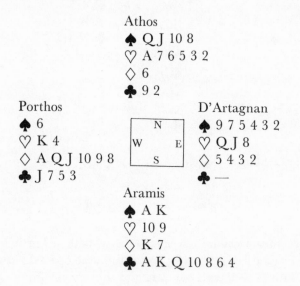

Athos
♠ Q J 10 8
♡ A 7 6 5 3 2
◇ 6
♣ 9 2

Porthos
♠ 6
♡ K 4
◇ A Q J 10 9 8
♣ J 7 5 3

D'Artagnan
♠ 9 7 5 4 3 2
♡ Q J 8
◇ 5 4 3 2
♣ —

Aramis
♠ A K
♡ 10 9
◇ K 7
♣ A K Q 10 8 6 4

The bidding:

North	East	South	West
Pass	Pass	1 ♣	1 ◇
1 ♡	Pass	2 NT	Pass
3 ♡	Pass	3 NT	

Quite inadvertently Porthos had put his ♡ K among his diamonds, and believing it to be the ◇ K he led it. Aramis did not see any purpose in ducking so he won with dummy's ace, d'Artagnan dropping the jack. Aramis now assumed the

Paris 23

lead to be from K–Q–8–4 and so played the ♠ 8 to the king, cashed the ♠ A and then topped the clubs. He was disappointed to find d'Artagnan void in clubs, but continued with a fourth club in the firm belief that Porthos could take only two hearts and the ◊ A. But winning with the ♣ J Porthos naturally played the ♡ 4. D'Artagnan cashed his two hearts and shifted to diamonds—and the contract was down three.

The deviousness of Aramis on the next deal was perfectly fair, but . . .

North/N–S.

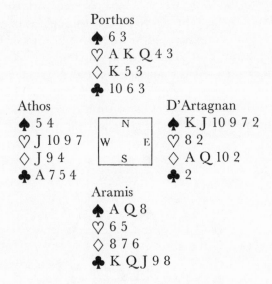

Porthos
♠ 6 3
♡ A K Q 4 3
◊ K 5 3
♣ 10 6 3

Athos
♠ 5 4
♡ J 10 9 7
◊ J 9 4
♣ A 7 5 4

D'Artagnan
♠ K J 10 9 7 2
♡ 8 2
◊ A Q 10 2
♣ 2

Aramis
♠ A Q 8
♡ 6 5
◊ 8 7 6
♣ K Q J 9 8

The bidding:

North	East	South	West
1 ♡	1 ♠	2 NT	Pass
3 ♡	Pass	3 NT	

Athos led the ♠ 5. D'Artagnan played the ♠ 9, and to induce his opponents to continue with spades Aramis won with the ace! In d'Artagnan's mind it looked as if Athos must hold the queen and had led from Q–8–5. As Aramis started playing clubs Athos was rather confused. If Aramis had had only one stopper in spades it was curious that he had not ducked at least once. For safety's sake Athos ducked twice, won the third club, and waited for an eventual signal from d'Artagnan who, however, discarded the ♡ 2 and the ◇ 2, for the good reason that he preferred Athos to continue with the ♠ Q rather than shift to a red suit. In these circumstances Athos continued with the ♠ 4 which enlightened d'Artagnan. Aramis laughed quietly to himself, but his laughter changed when d'Artagnan won with the ♠ K and shifted to the ♡ 8, which Athos covered with the ♡ 9. In order not to have his ◇ K played through at once Aramis had to win in dummy, but he had to lead hearts or diamonds from dummy, and so he went down two.

Before they left the musketeers told d'Artagnan about a hand from a small duplicate held in de Tréville's 'hotel' during the previous week between a dozen musketeers who had become tired of playing at war on a staircase landing.

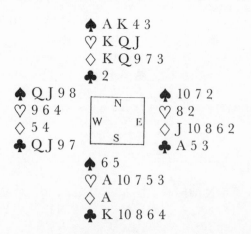

```
              ♠ A K 4 3
              ♡ K Q J
              ◇ K Q 9 7 3
              ♣ 2
♠ Q J 9 8        N        ♠ 10 7 2
♡ 9 6 4     W        E     ♡ 8 2
◇ 5 4            S        ◇ J 10 8 6 2
♣ Q J 9 7                 ♣ A 5 3
              ♠ 6 5
              ♡ A 10 7 5 3
              ◇ A
              ♣ K 10 8 6 4
```

'I was in 6 ♡ as South,' Athos said. 'A trump was led. I won in dummy and led the ♣ 2. East came up with the ace and continued trumps. Again I won in dummy, played the

◇ 3 to the ace in order to ruff a low club with the ♡ K, returned to the hand by ruffing a diamond and drew the outstanding trump. The two low clubs were discarded on dummy's ◇ K–Q . . .'

'It wasn't really as easy as you say,' Aramis interrupted. 'I was West at my table and led the ♠ Q. South led the club from dummy. My partner won with the ace and continued in spades, in this way depriving the declarer of his entry to the diamonds. Declarer had the idea that he could not cash the three diamond tricks before trumps had been drawn, but if he played three trumps ending in dummy he couldn't get a club ruffed, and would finish one trick short. So he played a diamond to the ace, cashed the ♣ K and ruffed the ♣ 6 with the ♡ J. On the ◇ K he threw the ♣ 8. He re-entered the closed hand by ruffing the ♠ 3 with the ♡ 3, ruffed the ♣ 10 with the ♡ Q and cashed the ♡ K. But when he tried to come back to the closed hand by another spade ruff East uppercut with the ♡ 8 compelling the declarer to overruff with the ♡ 10, so that my ♡ 9 was promoted to the setting trick. Thus the slam could not be made with a spade lead! And by the way, Porthos, what went on at your table?'

'Nothing much, except that *I* made 6 ♡ against a spade lead.'

'How on earth did you do that?' Aramis burst out.

'You know as well as I do, Aramis, that I like simple methods,' Porthos answered. 'I won with dummy's ♠ K and played the ♣ 2. East won and continued in spades. I won and played a diamond to the ace, ruffed a low club with the ♡ J, ruffed a low diamond, ruffed another club with the ♡ Q, cashed the ♡ K, ruffed a low spade and drew the last two trumps. The result was that I had two good clubs in the closed hand as well as the two highest diamonds in dummy, so it didn't matter where I was. Voila tout!'

Both Aramis and Athos were rather taken aback and exchanged glances. But they could find no flaw in Porthos' 'simple' method.

The keen rivalry and the resultant fights between the

King's musketeers and the Cardinal's guardsmen, from both of which the King and the Cardinal officially dissociated themselves but which, nevertheless, they privately encouraged, had taken a serious turn. The result was a duel between d'Artagnan, who was not yet a musketeer, and Bernajoux, one of the Cardinal's most loyal supporters and, moreover, one of his best swordsmen. D'Artagnan, it should be added, was constantly in the company of his three new friends. Excellent swordsman as he was Bernajoux could not compete with d'Artagnan's swiftness with *his* sword and unorthodox way of fighting. He was killed. This nearly meant disaster for d'Artagnan and his friends, but later when it had been confirmed to the King that Bernajoux had provoked the quarrel all four were restored to grace. They were even granted an audience, and the King gave d'Artagnan forty gold nobles. Porthos at once suggested that, since he was so well in funds, he should have a servant—and this led to d'Artagnan engaging Planchet.

That same night they all played at Athos' rooms in the rue Férou.

North/E–W.

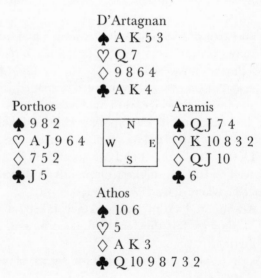

D'Artagnan
♠ A K 5 3
♡ Q 7
♢ 9 8 6 4
♣ A K 4

Porthos
♠ 9 8 2
♡ A J 9 6 4
♢ 7 5 2
♣ J 5

Aramis
♠ Q J 7 4
♡ K 10 8 3 2
♢ Q J 10
♣ 6

Athos
♠ 10 6
♡ 5
♢ A K 3
♣ Q 10 9 8 7 3 2

The bidding:

North	South
1 ♠	2 ♣
2 ♢	3 ♣
4 ♣	5 ♣

Porthos opened with the ♠ 9 and Athos ducked with the ♠ 3 in dummy. He was never afraid of chancing his arm with his opponents, and in this instance he saw no particular danger but even the possibility of an overtrick. Aramis won the trick with the ♠ J and shifted, as Athos had expected him to do, to diamonds—up to weakness.

Athos won with the ♢ A, played the ♣ 3 to the king, cashed the ♣ A dropping the ♣ 7, and played the ♢ 6 to the king. Then he brought in dummy with the ♠ 10 to the king, discarded the ♢ 3 on the ♠ A, and ruffed the ♢ 8 with the ♣ 8. All following suit the ♢ 9 was now good, and with his usual foresight Athos had held the ♣ 2 which he now played to dummy's ♣ 4 so as to throw the ♡ 5 on the ♢ 9 —with twelve tricks the result.

Of course, Athos could have cashed the ♣ Q first with exactly the same result, but it should be granted that the method he chose was neat and worthy of Athos.

South/E–W.

Aramis
♠ 7 5 4
♡ 6 2
◇ Q 7 2
♣ A Q 10 6 5

Porthos
♠ 8
♡ Q J 10 9 7 5
◇ 6 5 4
♣ 8 7 3

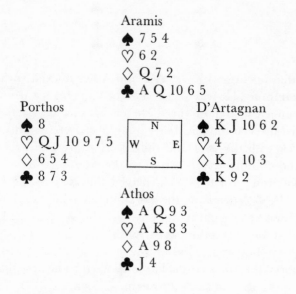

D'Artagnan
♠ K J 10 6 2
♡ 4
◇ K J 10 3
♣ K 9 2

Athos
♠ A Q 9 3
♡ A K 8 3
◇ A 9 8
♣ J 4

The bidding:

South	North
1 ♠	2 ♣
2 ♡	3 ♣
3 NT	

Porthos led the ♡ Q and Athos won with the king in order to play the ♣ J, and let it run. D'Artagnan held off hoping that Athos held only two clubs. The next trick d'Artagnan won with the king over dummy's ♣ 10, and shifted to the ♠ J which Athos took with the ♠ Q. Porthos followed with the ♠ 8 which looked like a singleton. But nevertheless Athos continued with the ♠ A and d'Artagnan, seeing that Athos intended to endplay him, followed with the ♠ 6. When Athos continued with the ♠ 9 d'Artagnan won with the ♠ 10 and exited with the ♠ 2! Three spade tricks along with the one club were not enough to set the contract.

Athos gave an approving nod, but was not going to give up. To find out who held the ◇ K he laid down his ◇ 9. Porthos, who had already discarded two diamonds, followed with the ◇ 6, and Athos played the ◇ 2 from dummy. But once more d'Artagnan was ready, and dropped the ◇ 3! If he had not ducked four tricks would again have been obtainable. Until now d'Artagnan had presented Athos with two tricks, but these were not one bit welcome as they blocked him from three club tricks in dummy. Three spade tricks, two heart tricks, two diamond tricks and one club trick made only eight tricks in all, and despite his very elegant play Athos had to go one down.

But as Athos said later, he could have made the contract if he had gone up with the ace on the second club.

South/Love all.

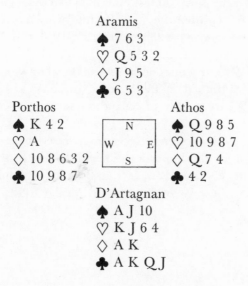

```
                    Aramis
                    ♠ 7 6 3
                    ♡ Q 5 3 2
                    ◇ J 9 5
                    ♣ 6 5 3
    Porthos                        Athos
    ♠ K 4 2          ┌─────────┐   ♠ Q 9 8 5
    ♡ A              │    N    │   ♡ 10 9 8 7
    ◇ 10 8 6 3 2     │ W     E │   ◇ Q 7 4
    ♣ 10 9 8 7       │    S    │   ♣ 4 2
                     └─────────┘
                    D'Artagnan
                    ♠ A J 10
                    ♡ K J 6 4
                    ◇ A K
                    ♣ A K Q J
```

Doubtless under the influence of his successful day d'Artagnan was remarkably optimistic in his bidding. And in this case he opened with 4 No Trumps! Aramis signed off with 5 ♣, but d'Artagnan followed up with 5 No Trumps! Aramis well understood d'Artagnan's mood of intoxication, and with his own poor hand he simply passed, which proved to be a wise move on his part.

5 No Trumps was, in fact, sufficient, and if Porthos had been able to find a diamond opening it would, indeed, have been too high, but in the event Porthos led the ♣ 10.

D'Artagnan won with the ♣ A and wondered what he should do next. To win it was perfectly clear that he needed three heart tricks and two spade tricks. If the spade honours were not both held by Porthos, then for the double finesse in spades dummy would have to supply two entries in hearts. The heart situation was certainly not all that could be desired but when d'Artagnan cashed all his clubs, throwing the ♠ 3 from dummy, Athos found himself in difficulties. He could not discard more than one spade for otherwise declarer needed only one spade finesse and so he had to let go a heart. Then d'Artagnan led the ♡ 6. Porthos won and led a diamond. Athos did not cover dummy's ◇ 9, but d'Artagnan could not duck. He cashed the ♡ K, took the ♡ J over with dummy's ♡ Q and finessed in spades. Porthos won with the king and continued in diamonds. Now d'Artagnan could lead the ♡ 4 to dummy's ♡ 5 and finesse spades once again to make the contract.

As will have been seen d'Artagnan in his younger days had a clear eye for the importance of minor details, for in the above hand he was well aware from the very beginning of the importance of the ♡ 4 as an essential bridge to the dummy.

South/Love all.

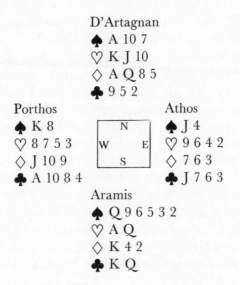

D'Artagnan
♠ A 10 7
♡ K J 10
◇ A Q 8 5
♣ 9 5 2

Porthos
♠ K 8
♡ 8 7 5 3
◇ J 10 9
♣ A 10 8 4

Athos
♠ J 4
♡ 9 6 4 2
◇ 7 6 3
♣ J 7 6 3

Aramis
♠ Q 9 6 5 3 2
♡ A Q
◇ K 4 2
♣ K Q

The bidding:

South	North
1 ♠	2 ◇
2 ♠	3 NT
4 ♠	6 ♠

In this hand Porthos opened with the ♣ A followed by the ♣ 4, and Aramis won with the king. He looked suspiciously at Porthos and remarked acidly, as if suspecting that Porthos had cashed his ace in the belief that he held a certain trump trick:

'Do you *always* lead aces against small slams?'

Aramis then led the ♠ Q. Porthos, of course, was not going to let himself be caught out by that and innocently followed with the ♠ 8, and in the next trick the ♠ K and the ♠ J fell resoundingly on the ace.

D'Artagnan's new servant had asked to be allowed to wait on the four players during their game. Permission was granted and they all noticed that he was making notes as he did so. They had no objection to his doing this, and, indeed, they added to his collection by telling him about hands they had played, and reserving for him those hands which he would have no opportunity to kibitz himself.

Planchet was perfectly happy in his work as long as the King's gold pieces lasted, but when these had been eaten (and drunk) up he started complaining. Whereupon d'Artagnan first gave him a good thrashing and then, to Planchet's great surprise, forbade him to leave his service. The reason for this was that d'Artagnan felt quite sure that his luck would turn, and, anyway, he was too good a master not to share his good luck with his servant. D'Artagnan was quite right in what he did for otherwise no one would ever have learned about the musketeers' exploits at the card-table.

D'Artagnan had, of course, told his newfound friends about the affair at Meung where he had had a difference of opinion with an unknown man who had had the very one-sided sympathy of the people at the inn. This man, it may be remembered, had stolen from an unconscious d'Artagnan his letter of introduction to de Tréville.

For the afternoon following the evening bridge session in the rue Férou Athos had arranged one of the small duplicates. Just as they were starting to play d'Artagnan happened to glance out of the window, and who should he see but the man from Meung crossing the street! He jumped up and ran to the door, sword in hand, with a shout to Grimaud who was aimlessly standing near the door:

'Play my cards, Grimaud.'

Grimaud looked at his master. Athos gave him a nod and Grimaud sat down and took up South's hand. The hands were:

South/Love all.

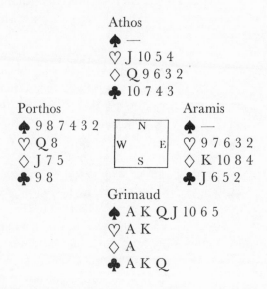

Athos
♠ —
♡ J 10 5 4
♢ Q 9 6 3 2
♣ 10 7 4 3

Porthos
♠ 9 8 7 4 3 2
♡ Q 8
♢ J 7 5
♣ 9 8

Aramis
♠ —
♡ 9 7 6 3 2
♢ K 10 8 4
♣ J 6 5 2

Grimaud
♠ A K Q J 10 6 5
♡ A K
♢ A
♣ A K Q

Just in case readers are not familiar with 'The Three Musketeers' it should be mentioned here that Athos had trained his personal servant to express himself by using certain signs and gestures, but only to speak when it was absolutely necessary. The consequence was that Grimaud behaved like a mute for most of the time. Now he was the dealer, and faithful to his habit, he made a gesture which he meant to be understood as a bid of 7 No Trumps, but which was misunderstood unfortunately by the other players as a pass. The three of them all passed and the hand was thrown in.

Needless to say Grimaud felt miserable, but didn't say a word. But all four passing, however, gave a pure top because the declarers in 7 No Trumps at the other tables went two down after a diamond lead.

Soon after this d'Artagnan returned having vainly sought for his enemy. It was only much later that he learned that the man was a henchman of the Cardinal and that he was, indeed, the comte de Rochefort.

D'Artagnan took over from Grimaud, and here are some of the afternoon's hands.

North/Love all.

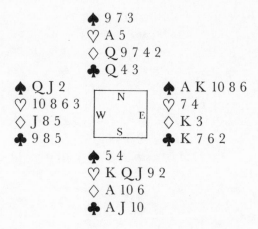

The bidding:

North	East	South	West
Pass	1 ♠	Dble.	Pass
2 ◇	Pass	2 ♡	Pass
3 ♡	Pass	4 ♡	

At all the tables West cashed the ♠ Q and J and continued with the ♠ 2.

Athos, as South, ruffed the third round with the ♡ 9, took the ♡ J over with dummy's ace so that he could play the ♣ Q and after three club tricks Athos cashed the ♡ K and Q and put West in with the ♡ 2. West had nothing but diamonds to lead and Athos reasoning that East held the king doubleton, it did not matter which diamond West led— Athos took all the diamond tricks.

It was d'Artagnan who told about this hand later in the evening; he had been dummy, and Porthos shook his head in amazement as he heard of the esoteric way of playing.

'Mordieux!' he exclaimed. 'There you are again. I could have done it in a much simpler way. To the fourth trick I would have laid down the ♢ 10 and let it run to East's king. East would have shifted to the ♣ 7, and even if I had thought that he held the ♣ K I would have needed no finesse. I would have won with the ace, cashed four trumps and the ♢ A, and then dummy's diamonds would have taken the rest!'

North/N–S.

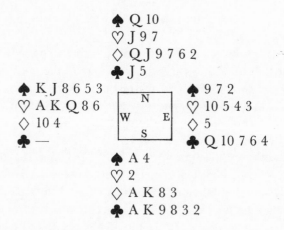

♠ Q 10
♡ J 9 7
♢ Q J 9 7 6 2
♣ J 5

♠ K J 8 6 5 3
♡ A K Q 8 6
♢ 10 4
♣ —

♠ 9 7 2
♡ 10 5 4 3
♢ 5
♣ Q 10 7 6 4

♠ A 4
♡ 2
♢ A K 8 3
♣ A K 9 8 3 2

The bidding:

North	East	South	West
Pass	Pass	1 ♣	1 ♠
Pass	Pass	3 ♢	3 ♡
4 ♢	4 ♡	6 ♢	

Against Athos the ♡ K was led followed by the ♡ A which Athos ruffed with the ♢ A. He cashed the ♢ K and led another trump to dummy in order to play the ♣ J which was covered by East with the ♣ Q, and won with the king. The last trump was led to dummy and trumps continued until this position was reached:

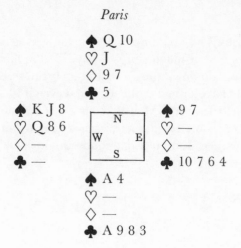

The ◇ 9 followed and East had to throw a spade in order to guard clubs. Athos threw the ♣ 3, took the club finesse, cashed the ♣ A and ruffed the last club. West had to blank the ♠ K and the ♡ Q. Dummy had the ♠ Q and the ♡ J, and Athos could now take the ♠ Q over with the ace and score the last trick with the ♠ 4.

At another table Aramis was leading against 6 ◇, and here it was not long before everything was over. He led the ♡ 6! Declarer might just as well have used dummy's ♡ J, but instead he played the ♡ 9. To his great surprise Porthos won the trick with the ♡ 10, but it was not too difficult for him to see what was going on—he shifted to a club, and the contract was down before the declarer could get in.

South/Both.

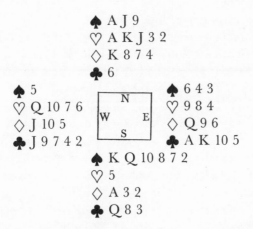

♠ A J 9
♡ A K J 3 2
♢ K 8 7 4
♣ 6

♠ 5
♡ Q 10 7 6
♢ J 10 5
♣ J 9 7 4 2

♠ 6 4 3
♡ 9 8 4
♢ Q 9 6
♣ A K 10 5

♠ K Q 10 8 7 2
♡ 5
♢ A 3 2
♣ Q 8 3

At two different tables Porthos and d'Artagnan were declarers in 6 ♠. Modern rules of opening leads were not known then, but it was rather a neat idea of West at both tables to lead his singleton ♠ 5.

Later in the evening, while Porthos twisted his moustache impatiently to tell about his own play, Athos spoke admiringly of how d'Artagnan had made the slam only after he had worked out every angle of approach. He had won the first trick with dummy's ♠ 9. With the trump lead it was impossible to have two clubs ruffed, but if the fifth heart could be set up, then one club ruff would be sufficient. This, however, presupposed a 2–2 trump break for which he could hardly hope. He therefore tried first of all another, and apparently better, possibility. He cashed the ♡ A and K, throwing the ♢ 2 and not a club. A heart ruff showed that the fifth heart could be established. However, before relying on the 2–2 trumps he tried the diamonds, first the ♢ A, then the ♢ K, and then he ruffed the ♢ 7, and as all followed suit the fourth diamond was good. It now only remained to play a trump to the ♠ J, ruff a heart with the ♠ Q, and enter dummy on the ♠ A, to discard two clubs on the ♡ J and the ♢ 8. East got the final trick on the ♣ A.

Paris

Porthos shook his head as he listened to this very complicated way of playing.

'You always make things so involved,' he said. 'It would
have been much easier if you had played the way I did. I won
the first trick in the closed hand with the ♠ 10 and immediately
finessed hearts. Then I ruffed a heart, drew the trumps and
discarded three losers on the good hearts.'

'That may be so,' d'Artagnan replied, 'but when you were
brave enough to finesse hearts why didn't you take the over-
trick? You might, as I did, have discarded a diamond and
ruffed the fourth diamond for your last losing card.'

For as long as the four friends could participate in
d'Artagnan's good fortune they continued to play at different
inns. On one particular occasion they spent a good part of
the night at a place named 'La Chevrette', and the following
is a selection of the hands played there. As a matter of fact
this inn to which d'Artagnan had taken such a liking was not
owned by the beautiful Madeleine until twenty years later.

The hands had been unexciting until the following one was
dealt. Athos' confidence in d'Artagnan's skill showed in his
bidding here for a very close contract.

East/Love all.

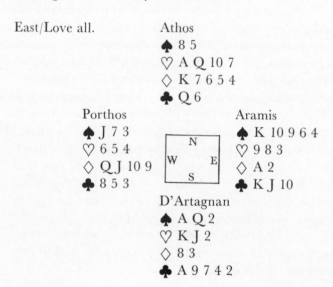

Athos
♠ 8 5
♡ A Q 10 7
◇ K 7 6 5 4
♣ Q 6

Porthos
♠ J 7 3
♡ 6 5 4
◇ Q J 10 9
♣ 8 5 3

Aramis
♠ K 10 9 6 4
♡ 9 8 3
◇ A 2
♣ K J 10

D'Artagnan
♠ A Q 2
♡ K J 2
◇ 8 3
♣ A 9 7 4 2

The bidding:

East	South	West	North
1 ♠	2 ♣	Pass	2 ♡
Pass	2 NT	Pass	3 NT

With his strong diamond sequence Porthos thought, naturally, that it would be a good idea to lead from this suit and he did with the ◇ Q. From his point of view this was not a dangerous thing to do, but it was just that straw in the wind which helped d'Artagnan to make the contract which would have been hopeless if a spade had been led. When Aramis followed with the ◇ 2 Porthos quickly shifted to the ♠ J, and he won this trick too. He continued with the ♠ 7, but d'Artagnan won with the ♠ Q and then led the ◇ 8, ducking with the ◇ 5 in dummy. As he expected, Aramis had to win with the ace and lost an entry. The rest of the play was a walk-over for d'Artagnan. He won the next trick with the ♠ A, took the ♡ J over with the queen in dummy, cashed the ◇ K and lost a diamond to Porthos, but the fifth diamond was good. Thus d'Artagnan made the contract with two tricks in spades, four in hearts, two in diamonds and one club.

Although it is a golden rule for the defenders not to fool around too much between the suits, Porthos could still have set the contract if he had shifted again in the third trick—to clubs! But d'Artagnan did not, of course, let him know this.

A short time later Athos had the opportunity to prove that he was never afraid of giving his opponents the chance to show their mettle.

East/Both.

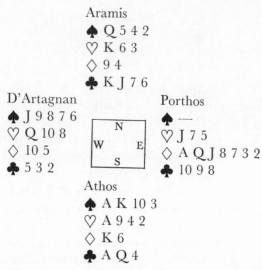

Aramis
♠ Q 5 4 2
♡ K 6 3
◇ 9 4
♣ K J 7 6

D'Artagnan
♠ J 9 8 7 6
♡ Q 10 8
◇ 10 5
♣ 5 3 2

Porthos
♠ —
♡ J 7 5
◇ A Q J 8 7 3 2
♣ 10 9 8

Athos
♠ A K 10 3
♡ A 9 4 2
◇ K 6
♣ A Q 4

Porthos opened the bidding with 3 ◇, but Athos bought the contract at 4 ♠, and d'Artagnan led the ◇ 10. Athos won the second trick with the ◇ K and was glad that he had not gone after the slam, if only for the reason that having played the ♠ K he found Porthos void in trumps. It would have been easy enough to play three rounds of clubs as well as three rounds of hearts, for even if Porthos should have won the third heart d'Artagnan would have had to ruff his next lead and play trumps into the declarer's tenace. However, Athos thought that this was too simple and, instead, worked out some pretty play both for himself and d'Artagnan, playing *four* rounds of clubs and ruffing the last club with the ♠ A! D'Artagnan was up to the situation and underruffed with the ♠ 7!! When Athos then continued with three rounds of hearts d'Artagnan unblocked the queen and then, thanks to the undertrumping, allowed Porthos to win the third heart. Porthos now had nothing but diamonds to play, and Athos threw his last heart. It was now that d'Artagnan had to ruff with the ♠ 8, and it was Athos who underruffed with dummy's ♠ 4!

Despite his valiant defence d'Artagnan was helpless—he had to lead away from ♠ J–9 into the combined tenace, for ♠ Q–5 was in dummy and ♠ 10–3 in the closed hand.

D'Artagnan remarked in an aside to Athos: 'You were very nearly too kind-hearted, but when you are as resourceful as that you were perfectly entitled to play as you did.'

South/N–S with partscore 30.

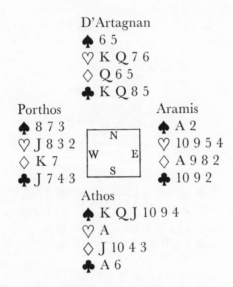

D'Artagnan
♠ 6 5
♡ K Q 7 6
♢ Q 6 5
♣ K Q 8 5

Porthos
♠ 8 7 3
♡ J 8 3 2
♢ K 7
♣ J 7 4 3

Aramis
♠ A 2
♡ 10 9 5 4
♢ A 9 8 2
♣ 10 9 2

Athos
♠ K Q J 10 9 4
♡ A
♢ J 10 4 3
♣ A 6

Athos opened the bidding with 1 ♠, d'Artagnan bid 1 No Trumps and Athos 3 ♠, followed by three passes.

Porthos was aware that unusual methods were required to set the contract so, rather recklessly, he led the ♢ K. Aramis echoed with the ♢ 9 and won the next trick with the ♢ A. The question now was whether to return the ♢ 8 or the ♢ 2. According to the Mauléon convention, which we now call the Lavinthal signal, the first meant that he wanted Porthos to play a heart, while the ♢ 2 meant that he wanted a club; but, in fact, he wanted neither hearts nor clubs—and solved the problem by leading both the ♢ 8 and the ♢ 2.

It was not in Athos' nature to claim a penalty but,

naturally enough, he asked Aramis to take one of the cards
back. Resignedly Aramis shuffled the two cards and played
one of them at random. It proved to be the ◇ 8; on his own
accord he placed the ◇ 2 on the table as penalty card.
Porthos ruffed believing that Athos must hold both the ♡ A
and the ♣ A since Aramis would not use the Mauléon signal.
The only chance, therefore, was that Aramis *might* hold the
♠ A, so Porthos led the ♠ 3. Aramis won with the ♠ A, and
'in his own opinion' had no choice but to lead the penalty
card, the ◇ 2. So Porthos got another ruff and the contract
went one down.

South/Both.

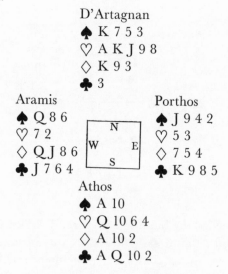

D'Artagnan
♠ K 7 5 3
♡ A K J 9 8
◇ K 9 3
♣ 3

Aramis
♠ Q 8 6
♡ 7 2
◇ Q J 8 6
♣ J 7 6 4

Porthos
♠ J 9 4 2
♡ 5 3
◇ 7 5 4
♣ K 9 8 5

Athos
♠ A 10
♡ Q 10 6 4
◇ A 10 2
♣ A Q 10 2

The bidding:

South	North
1 NT	2 ♣
2 ♡	4 NT
5 ♠	7 ♡

Aramis opened with the ◇ J. Athos won with the ace in
the closed hand and played the ♡ 4 to dummy's king, saying
to Aramis as he did so:

'I know only too well that you do not lead a jack as the 'top of nothing'. So it was a bluff lead from Q–J, and the contract is cold if I finesse your queen. However, I will give you another chance.'

He played the singleton ♣ 3 and finessed with the queen. He could now have discarded a diamond from dummy on the ♣ 4 and cross-ruffed clubs and spades, but said instead:

'This is all too easy. All the same I will prove what I said about your ◇ Q.'

He led the ◇ 10 and let it run, but despite the opportunities he had given the two musketeers they were unable to set the contract.

East/Love all.

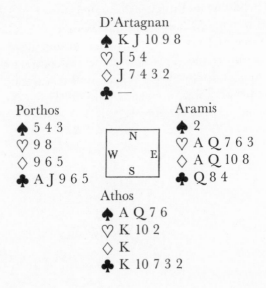

D'Artagnan
♠ K J 10 9 8
♡ J 5 4
◇ J 7 4 3 2
♣ —

Porthos
♠ 5 4 3
♡ 9 8
◇ 9 6 5
♣ A J 9 6 5

Aramis
♠ 2
♡ A Q 7 6 3
◇ A Q 10 8
♣ Q 8 4

Athos
♠ A Q 7 6
♡ K 10 2
◇ K
♣ K 10 7 3 2

The bidding:

East	South	West	North
1 ♡	1 ♠	2 ♣	2 ♠
3 ♣	Dble.	Pass	4 ♠

Porthos opened with the ♡ 9 which was taken by Aramis with the ace and then followed by the ♡ 7 which Athos won with the ♡ 10. Even if Athos was now aware that Porthos could ruff a heart he led the ◇ K! Aramis was pleased to win with the ◇ A and led a heart for Porthos to ruff, but this was their last trick even if Porthos shifted to a trump. Athos let dummy win with the ♠ 8 and cross-ruffed three diamonds from duumy and three clubs from the closed hand, after which dummy's ◇ J was good.

Planchet's apt comment to this hand was: 'That was a fine example of turning the time factor to its full advantage.'

Somewhere Alexandre Dumas has stated that Aramis never gambled. That is not strictly correct. Athos and Porthos played dice, and Dumas relates how on one occasion Aramis played dice with Porthos (it was at 'Le Colombier-Rouge') while Athos listening through a stove pipe heard the Cardinal instruct Milady about her voyage to England. But what Dumas did not know was that Aramis liked playing bridge, or rather the game now known as contract bridge—he was, indeed, quite a good player, and it was more than a pity that his play was often spoiled by following the maxim that the end justifies the means.

South/N–S.

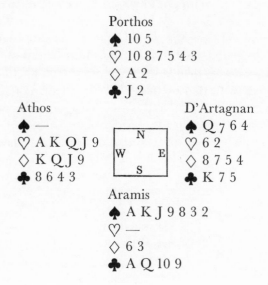

Porthos
♠ 10 5
♡ 10 8 7 5 4 3
♢ A 2
♣ J 2

Athos
♠ —
♡ A K Q J 9
♢ K Q J 9
♣ 8 6 4 3

D'Artagnan
♠ Q 7 6 4
♡ 6 2
♢ 8 7 5 4
♣ K 7 5

Aramis
♠ A K J 9 8 3 2
♡ —
♢ 6 3
♣ A Q 10 9

The bidding:

South	West	North	East
1 ♠	Dble.	Pass	1 NT
3 ♣	3 ♢	3 NT	Pass
4 ♢	Dble.	Redble.	Pass
5 ♣	Pass	5 ♠	Pass
7 ♠	Dble.	Pass	Pass
Redble.			

While Athos was pondering over what to lead Aramis changed hands with the inquisitive Porthos, and when Athos had led the ♡ K it was Aramis who spread the dummy. Aramis ruffed. His scheme had already been thought out before he put dummy down and so, with little hesitation, he led the ♢ 3. Athos, who saw only the A–2 on the table, played the ♢ 9. Aramis fumbled with the ♢ 2, and then the ♢ 10 which had been hidden under the ♢ 2 came up. He won the trick with it, which meant not only an extra trick but also an extra entry which was necessary to finesse both spades and clubs. With both finesses succeeding he made the redoubled grand slam.

Until now this was the shabbiest thing he had done, and d'Artagnan glared at him. But Athos hastened to say:

'It really was my own fault. There was no reason for me to be so greedy with that diamond.'

Another example of Aramis' methods to make dubious contracts was to abuse his knowledge of the rules. In the next hand it was a lead out of turn that gave him the chance.

North/Both.

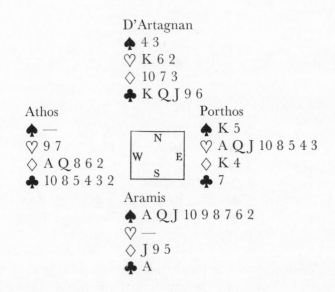

D'Artagnan
♠ 4 3
♡ K 6 2
◇ 10 7 3
♣ K Q J 9 6

Athos
♠ —
♡ 9 7
◇ A Q 8 6 2
♣ 10 8 5 4 3 2

Porthos
♠ K 5
♡ A Q J 10 8 5 4 3
◇ K 4
♣ 7

Aramis
♠ A Q J 10 9 8 7 6 2
♡ —
◇ J 9 5
♣ A

The biddings:

North	East	South	West
Pass	1 ♡	4 ♠	Pass
Pass	5 ♡	5 ♠	6 ♡
Pass	Pass	6 ♠	Dble.

Could you believe that Aramis could make this slam because poor Porthos, quite unwittingly, led the ♣ 7 out of turn?

Aramis chose to treat the ♣ 7 as a penalty card with the result that Athos could lead whatever he wished; he was unlucky to choose his partner's suit, leading the ♡ 9. Aramis put on dummy's king to compel Porthos to use his ♡ A, and from the closed hand Aramis jettisoned the ♣ A! Now Porthos had to play the penalty card ♣ 7. Aramis dropped the ◇ 5, won with dummy's ♣ 9 and continued with the ♣ K. Porthos ruffed with the ♠ 5, but was overruffed by Aramis who drew the king with the ace and re-entered dummy with the ♠ 2 to the ♠ 4 in order to get rid of his remaining two diamond losers on the good clubs.

Once again Athos generously lost a trick which looked a gift to the opponents; later on it proved to have been a good investment:

South/Love all.

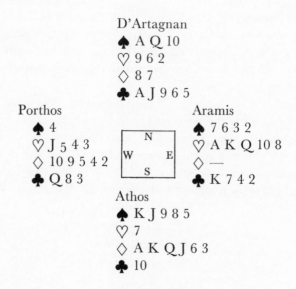

D'Artagnan
♠ A Q 10
♡ 9 6 2
◇ 8 7
♣ A J 9 6 5

Porthos
♠ 4
♡ J 5 4 3
◇ 10 9 5 4 2
♣ Q 8 3

Aramis
♠ 7 6 3 2
♡ A K Q 10 8
◇ —
♣ K 7 4 2

Athos
♠ K J 9 8 5
♡ 7
◇ A K Q J 6 3
♣ 10

The bidding:

South	West	North	East
1 ◇	Pass	2 ♣	2 ♡
2 ♠	Pass	3 ♣	3 ♡
3 ♠	Pass	4 ♠	5 ♡
Pass	Pass	5 ♠	

Porthos opened with the ♡ 3. Aramis won with the ♡ Q and continued with the ♡ K. Athos ruffed with the ♠ 8 and led the ♠ 5 to dummy's queen in order to lead a diamond from dummy. If everyone had followed suit Athos could have drawn all the trumps, and then the diamonds were good— but Aramis threw a club. Athos won with the ◇ K and then laid down the ◇ A! Aramis then ruffed with the ♠ 3 and led the ♡ 10. After Athos had shortened Aramis' trumps by the diamond ruff he could afford now to be shortened himself—he ruffed with the ♠ 9, ruffed the ◇ 3 with dummy's ♠ A, took the ♠ 10 over with the ♠ J, drew Aramis' last trump and took the rest.

Had Athos gone straight after the trumps the bad diamond distribution would have prevented him from making the contract. So he not only risked a diamond ruff by Aramis but even provoked it in order to be sure to maintain control of the trumps.

Even if the declarer has worked out a careful playing plan after the bidding it often happens that new situations crop up during play, thus compelling the declarer to alter his approach. No one could be more aware of this sort of thing happening than d'Artagnan, and this is shown in a hand he played nearly a week later at the inn 'La Pomme de Pin'.

South/N–S.

Athos
♠ K 10 6 3
♡ 10 9 3 2
♢ J 9 8 2
♣ 10

Porthos
♠ Q 8 5
♡ Q 8 7 5
♢ Q 10 6 4
♣ 8 5

Aramis
♠ J 7 2
♡ A 6 4
♢ 3
♣ Q J 9 6 4 3

D'Artagnan
♠ A 9 4
♡ K J
♢ A K 7 5
♣ A K 7 2

D'Artagnan opened the bidding with 2 No Trumps and Athos bid 3 No Trumps. It could almost have been modern Goren, but even if the necessary honour points were there to justify the bidding there arose a problem which was up to a player of d'Artagnan's calibre to solve to make the contract.

Porthos led the ♣ 8, and d'Artagnan won with the ace over Aramis' ♣ J. He then played three rounds of diamonds from top, Porthos winning with the ♢ Q and Aramis dropping a heart and a club. Porthos continued with the ♣ 5 and Aramis played the ♣ 9, costing d'Artagnan's king. He then led the last diamond to dummy in order to lead the ♠ 3 and finesse with the ♠ 9. Porthos won with the ♠ Q, but gave nothing away for he could exit in spades. D'Artagnan took the trick with the ace and played another spade to the king. This was the situation:

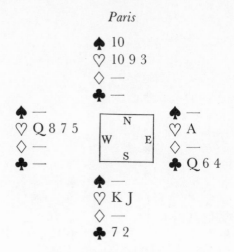

When the ♠ 10 was led from dummy East and West were caught in a curious endplay. Aramis threw a club and d'Artagnan the ♡ J. No matter what the heart distribution was d'Artagnan simply had to get another trick. If Aramis held the queen and Porthos the ace, Porthos would even have to let d'Artagnan hold the next trick with the ♡ K so as not to give dummy the two last tricks. But if Porthos held the A–Q he would get them both, but he would have to give dummy the last trick with the ♡ 10. In reality Aramis could take the ♡ A and the ♣ Q, but he would have to give d'Artagnan the last trick with the ♣ 7.

Now, Aramis was destined for the church. He was a good-looking young man and popular with ladies of high birth. One night when he was reading Augustin to one of his favourites he was threatened with a thrashing by a nobleman who was also interested in this particular lady. As a consequence of this Aramis took fencing lessons, in due course challenged the nobleman and duly killed him. That was why he had to give up his religious studies, at least temporarily, and become a musketeer. However, during the period of his religious instruction he had had time to absorb a great many of his particular teachings, and, rather unfortunately, carry them into practice at the bridge table.

It should, perhaps, be mentioned here that the four men were still playing at the 'Pomme de Pin'.

East/N–S.

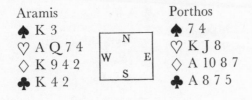

	Aramis			Porthos
♠	K 3		♠	7 4
♡	A Q 7 4		♡	K J 8
◇	K 9 4 2		◇	A 10 8 7
♣	K 4 2		♣	A 8 7 5

The bidding: East   West

                    1 ◇   1 ♡
                    1 NT   3 NT

'Porthos,' Aramis called out after three passes, 'let me see your cards,' and at the same time he gave Porthos his own cards just as South led the ♠ Q. It took no time for Aramis to see that the contract was hopeless with the ♠ A in North —and yet! Without a moment's hesitation he spread with a rapid movement East's cards on the table as the dummy, in doing so making the ♠ K safe and sound for the ninth trick.

In the next hand when Aramis preferred to play the hand himself in 6 ♠ instead of supporting Porthos to 6 ♣ (or even to 7 ♣) it was partly because of the 150 honours and partly owing to his lack of partnership confidence.

North/N–S.

Porthos
♠ —
♡ A K 7 3
◇ 8 5
♣ A 9 8 6 4 3 2

D'Artagnan
♠ 9 8 6
♡ Q J 10 9 8
◇ 10 3 2
♣ K 7

Athos
♠ 7 5 4 3 2
♡ 6 5 2
◇ K Q J 9
♣ 5

Aramis
♠ A K Q J 10
♡ 4
◇ A 7 6 4
♣ Q J 10

The bidding:

North	South
1 ♣	2 ♠
3 ♣	3 ♠
4 ♡	6 ♠

D'Artagnan opened with the ♡ Q and this made Aramis ponder over the two chances there seemed to be of making the contract. He might either win with the ♡ K, ruff a low heart, cash the four high trumps and lose a club, since otherwise his three club honours blocked the suit—but this plan depended upon the trumps being 4–4. The other possibility was to hope to find the ♣ K with d'Artagnan and finesse it, but to be able to unblock the club honours on the ♡ A–K he had to allow d'Artagnan to hold the first heart trick. Should d'Artagnan then continue in hearts he could win with the king and unblock one of the clubs, pass to the closed hand on the ◇ A to draw five rounds of trumps, finesse clubs and, if d'Artagnan covered the queen with the king, win with the ace and unblock the last club on the ♡ A.

The trumps being, in fact, 5–3 it was perfectly correct for Aramis to work his second plan, and all would have been well if d'Artagnan had continued with hearts or diamonds, or even the ♣ 7. But d'Artagnan had foreseen Aramis' intentions and in the second trick shifted to the ♣ K! That upset the apple-cart, for it was no longer possible to make the contract. So Aramis played to go down at as cheap a price as possible by discarding two diamonds on the ♡ A–K, entering the closed hand on the ◇ A and drawing trumps. But he had to lose a diamond in the end.

D'Artagnan's greatest wish was to become a King's Musketeer. This was not immediately possible, but de Tréville asked his brother-in-law, Captain des Essarts, to enrol him for the time being in the Royal Guard. His duties were not particularly heavy and he could still spend a great deal of his time with his three friends. Moreover, whenever the three musketeers were sent out of Paris on some mission or other for de Tréville he could quite easily get leave of absence to accompany them. The first occasion was when they were north of Paris and put up for the night at the Hotel 'Le Dauphin d'Or' at Villers-Cotterets, where, in fact, Alexandre Dumas was born. The four of them had time for a couple of rubbers.

On one of their first deals Athos, as so often on earlier or later occasions, closed the auction with a bid which showed his unshaken confidence in d'Artagnan. As usual this young man was up to the occasion.

East/Both.

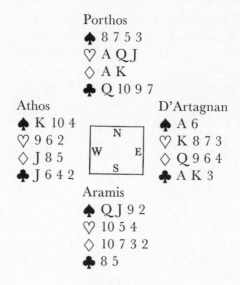

Porthos
♠ 8 7 5 3
♡ A Q J
◇ A K
♣ Q 10 9 7

Athos
♠ K 10 4
♡ 9 6 2
◇ J 8 5
♣ J 6 4 2

D'Artagnan
♠ A 6
♡ K 8 7 3
◇ Q 9 6 4
♣ A K 3

Aramis
♠ Q J 9 2
♡ 10 5 4
◇ 10 7 3 2
♣ 8 5

The bidding:

East	South	West	North
1 NT	Pass	Pass	Dble.
Pass	2 ♠	Dble.	

Athos led the ♣ 2, and dummy's ♣ 9 cost d'Artagnan's ♣ K. It was clear that Athos' double was within a hair's breadth, and d'Artagnan found the only next lead which could set the contract—he shifted to the ♡ 3! Dummy won with the ♡ J and led the ♠ 3. D'Artagnan followed with the ♠ 6, Aramis with the ♠ J and Athos, winning with the ♠ K, led the ♡ 6. With these repeated heart leads Aramis was unable to establish a club in time for a heart discard—so he tried finessing with the ♡ Q, but d'Artagnan won with the ♡ K and continued with the ♡ 7 to dummy's ace. He won the next trick with the ♠ A, cashed the ♣ A and then led the thirteenth heart. Whatever Aramis did Athos had to win a trick with the ♠ 10.

Planchet made notes on the next hand which was rather
an ordinary one for a player who kept his head. Average
players might misplay it, but it can readily be believed that
for Athos it was simply child's play.

South/E–W.

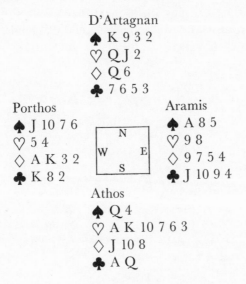

D'Artagnan
♠ K 9 3 2
♡ Q J 2
♢ Q 6
♣ 7 6 5 3

Porthos
♠ J 10 7 6
♡ 5 4
♢ A K 3 2
♣ K 8 2

Aramis
♠ A 8 5
♡ 9 8
♢ 9 7 5 4
♣ J 10 9 4

Athos
♠ Q 4
♡ A K 10 7 6 3
♢ J 10 8
♣ A Q

The bidding:

South	North
1 ♡	2 ♡
4 ♡	

After winning the first two tricks in diamonds Porthos
shifted to the ♡ 5, which Athos took with dummy's ♡ J.
Without knowing East's and West's cards most players
would probably draw another trump and try the club
finesse—and curse their bad luck. But Athos immediately led
the ♠ 2 from dummy! Aramis had to duck in order not to
make it too easy. Athos won with the ♠ Q and continued
with the ♠ 4. Porthos played the ♠ 10 and was allowed to
hold the trick. He exited with the ♡ 4 to dummy's queen.

The ♠ 9 was led, Aramis had to follow with the ace which Athos promptly ruffed. Then he created another entry to dummy by ruffing the good ◇ J with the ♡ 2 and threw the ♣ Q on the ♠ K which was now high. If the ♠ A had not appeared the club finesse was still open as the last chance, but why finesse as long as there are other possibilities?

In deciding his play in the next deal Aramis' conjecture about Porthos was correct, but he could not follow d'Artagnan's line of thought.

South/N–S.

Athos
♠ A 9 8 7
♡ 7 5 3
◇ A Q J
♣ A J 10

D'Artagnan
♠ K J 4
♡ Q J 10 4
◇ 6 4
♣ 6 5 4 3

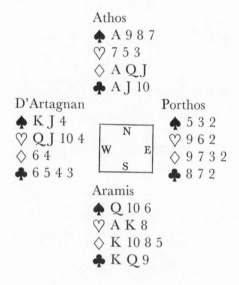

Porthos
♠ 5 3 2
♡ 9 6 2
◇ 9 7 3 2
♣ 8 7 2

Aramis
♠ Q 10 6
♡ A K 8
◇ K 10 8 5
♣ K Q 9

The bidding:	South	North
	1 NT	6 NT

D'Artagnan opened with the ♡ Q. Aramis won with the king and he saw plainly that he needed three spade tricks. He was undoubtedly aware that his best chance was the double finesse through West. But it was Porthos who sat East and Aramis was perfectly convinced that if Porthos held the ♠ K he would put it up on a small spade from dummy. So Aramis led a low diamond to dummy in order to play the ♠ 7, and when Porthos followed with the ♠ 2 Aramis finessed with the ♠ 10 which d'Artagnan took with the king! D'Artagnan had seen through Aramis' intentions and knew that if he won with the ♠ J then Aramis would finesse his king later. D'Artagnan continued with the ♡ J and this Aramis took with the ♡ A. Now it seemed perfectly clear to Aramis that Porthos must hold the ♠ J. So he again entered dummy in diamonds in order to lead the ♠ 8 and let it run. But he pulled a very long face indeed when d'Artagnan won with the ♠ J and cashed two hearts, setting the contract three times.

On another occasion when business entailed a journey to the south-east of Paris d'Artagnan had the chance to show his friends the Hotel 'Le Franc-Meunier' at Meung, where on his way to Paris on his dun-coloured horse he had his encounter with de Rochefort and had his first glimpse of Milady.

Inevitably bridge was played, and several interesting hands turned up.

South/Both.

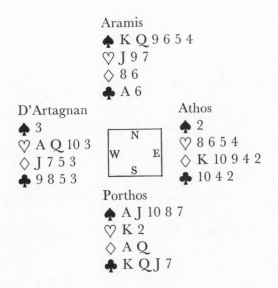

Aramis
♠ K Q 9 6 5 4
♡ J 9 7
♢ 8 6
♣ A 6

D'Artagnan
♠ 3
♡ A Q 10 3
♢ J 7 5 3
♣ 9 8 5 3

Athos
♠ 2
♡ 8 6 5 4
♢ K 10 9 4 2
♣ 10 4 2

Porthos
♠ A J 10 8 7
♡ K 2
♢ A Q
♣ K Q J 7

The bidding:

	South	North
	1 ♠	3 ♠
	4 NT	5 ◇
	6 ♠	

D'Artagnan led the ♣ 9 ,which Porthos won with dummy's ace. After a round of trumps Porthos began wondering what he should throw from dummy on the two long clubs, and moreover, what side suit he should develop. Unfortunately he could not throw all three hearts, so he decided to discard a heart and a diamond. Then he entered dummy with a trump in order to lead a heart to the king. D'Artagnan won two heart tricks, and Porthos went one down.

'I always guess wrong,' Porthos lamented.

'You shouldn't guess at all,' was d'Artagnan's answer. 'Don't ever base everything on one suit, but try two. Discard two hearts on the clubs and then you can play from dummy without the risk of losing two hearts. If Athos should be holding the ace you can get rid of one of dummy's diamonds on the ♡ K, and should I show up with the ♡ A you still have the chance of a lucky diamond finesse.'

South/N–S.

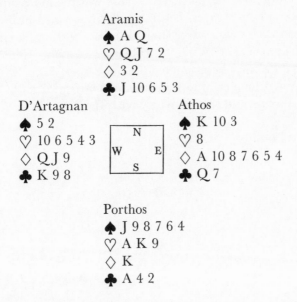

Aramis
♠ A Q
♡ Q J 7 2
◇ 3 2
♣ J 10 6 5 3

D'Artagnan
♠ 5 2
♡ 10 6 5 4 3
◇ Q J 9
♣ K 9 8

Athos
♠ K 10 3
♡ 8
◇ A 10 8 7 6 5 4
♣ Q 7

Porthos
♠ J 9 8 7 6 4
♡ A K 9
◇ K
♣ A 4 2

The bidding:

South	West	North	East
1 ♠	Pass	2 ♣	2 ◇
3 ♣	3 ◇	4 ♠	5 ◇
5 ♠			

D'Artagnan led the ◇ Q. Athos won with the ace and continued with a low diamond, which was duly ruffed by Porthos who led a trump to the queen. Athos won with the king and led a diamond to a ruff and discard. Porthos cheerfully ruffed with dummy's ♠ A, but when he had re-entered the closed hand on the ♡ K and laid down the ♠ J, the ♠ 10 did not fall. However, Porthos had enough common sense to lose the trump trick at once so that he could, undisturbed, discard his second low club on the fourth heart and only go down one.

Athos, of course, was well aware that if Porthos had two

low clubs he could not get rid of them both if he had shifted to clubs; but the defence he chose was the more interesting and without danger, because if Porthos ruffed in the closed hand there was nothing he could discard from dummy with advantage, and when he ruffed in dummy Athos' ♠ 10 would always be promoted.

What happened to Porthos in the next deal could happen to anyone, but seldom with such a lucky result.

West/Both.

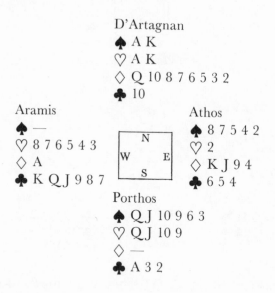

D'Artagnan
♠ A K
♡ A K
◇ Q 10 8 7 6 5 3 2
♣ 10

Aramis
♠ —
♡ 8 7 6 5 4 3
◇ A
♣ K Q J 9 8 7

Athos
♠ 8 7 5 4 2
♡ 2
◇ K J 9 4
♣ 6 5 4

Porthos
♠ Q J 10 9 6 3
♡ Q J 10 9
◇ —
♣ A 3 2

The bidding:

West	North	East	South
1 ♡	3 ◇	Pass	3 ♠
4 ♣	4 ◇	Pass	4 ♠
5 ♣	6 ♠		

Aramis led the ◇ A. Porthos intended to ruff with the ♠ 2, but pulled the wrong card—the ♣ 2—and that was that. Aramis shifted to the ♣ K and this time Porthos was more careful. He won with the ace and ruffed his last club with the ♠ K. Then having cashed the ♠ A he ruffed a diamond and drew all the trumps, taking care to unblock the two hearts from dummy so that he could make the four last tricks with the four hearts in the closed hand. When his friends congratulated him on his ingenious discard to the first trick he never batted an eyelid, but he well understood that he would have gone down if he had ruffed the ◇ A. Should he have later on ruffed a club, and used another ruff to re-enter the closed hand, Athos would have held one trump more than he could draw.

At some later date the four men called in at the Hotel 'La Belle-Etoile' in the rue de Bressac, which is now the rue de l'Arbre-Sec. They had only known of it by hearsay, but about fifty years earlier it had been a favourite meeting-place of two famous characters in Dumas' 'La Reine Margot'—La Mole and Coconnas. It was a comfortable enough hotel and it was not long before, once again, the cards were on the table.

East/Both.

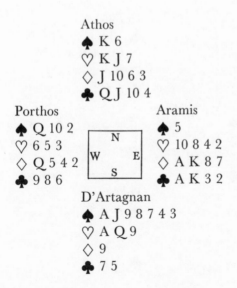

Athos
♠ K 6
♡ K J 7
◇ J 10 6 3
♣ Q J 10 4

Porthos
♠ Q 10 2
♡ 6 5 3
◇ Q 5 4 2
♣ 9 8 6

Aramis
♠ 5
♡ 10 8 4 2
◇ A K 8 7
♣ A K 3 2

D'Artagnan
♠ A J 9 8 7 4 3
♡ A Q 9
◇ 9
♣ 7 5

The bidding:

East	South	West	North
1 ◇	2 ♠	Pass	2 NT
Pass	4 ♠		

Porthos led the ◇ 2. Aramis won with the ◇ K and continued with the ◇ A, which d'Artagnan promptly ruffed. He then laid down the ♠ A and continued with the ♠ 4 to dummy's king in order to lead the ◇ J on which he threw the ♡ 9 from the closed hand. A cleverer man than Porthos might have been taken in by this discard, but in any event Porthos believed that hearts were the weak link so he shifted to the ♡ 6. And this was just what d'Artagnan needed. He won with the ♡ A, took the ♡ Q over with dummy's king and threw his two club losers on the ♡ J and the ◇ 10.

If, however, d'Artagnan should have got a similar hand in one of the two or three next deals he would discard a club, for Porthos would not then fall in the same trap so quickly.

North/Both.

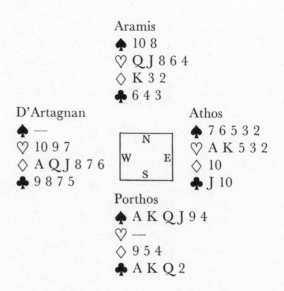

Aramis
♠ 10 8
♡ Q J 8 6 4
◇ K 3 2
♣ 6 4 3

D'Artagnan
♠ —
♡ 10 9 7
◇ A Q J 8 7 6
♣ 9 8 7 5

Athos
♠ 7 6 5 3 2
♡ A K 5 3 2
◇ 10
♣ J 10

Porthos
♠ A K Q J 9 4
♡ —
◇ 9 5 4
♣ A K Q 2

The bidding:

North	East	South	West
Pass	1 ♡	4 ♠	Pass
Pass	Dble.		

D'Artagnan led the ◊ A and continued with the ◊ Q. Athos ruffed dummy's king and exited with a trump. Porthos lost a trick each in diamonds and clubs and went one down.

Afterwards Porthos asked: 'Could I have made it?'

And d'Artagnan replied: 'Yes, very easily. When dummy's ♠ 8 won the third trick you should have led the ♡ Q, which Athos had to cover. Then you should have ruffed with the ♠ J, led the ♠ 9 to dummy and continued with the ♡ J. And again Athos would have to cover. You would then ruff and draw the last two trumps. On the last trump I would have to let go the ♡ 10 as I must keep the highest diamond and the four clubs. You would then have cashed the ♣ Q and endplayed Athos with the ♣ 2. Athos would have been forced to play hearts into dummy's tenace and, voilà, dummy would have taken the rest of the tricks!'

'And you call that easy?'

'Of course, because you would have had no use for the ♣ A and the ♣ K which you would have thrown on dummy's hearts!'

Variety is the spice of life and one evening the four of them decided to look in at the 'Hotel de la Barbe-Peinte', known to admirers of Dumas from his 'The Count of Moret' and 'The Red Sphinx'.

South/N–S.

Porthos
♠ 5 4 2
♡ K 10
♢ A Q 9 8 7
♣ 7 6 3

Aramis
♠ 6 3
♡ A 7 5 3
♢ 5
♣ 10 9 8 5 4 2

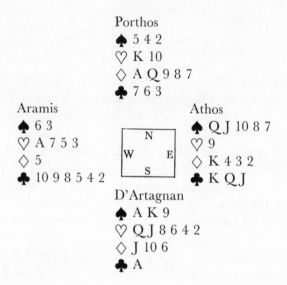

Athos
♠ Q J 10 8 7
♡ 9
♢ K 4 3 2
♣ K Q J

D'Artagnan
♠ A K 9
♡ Q J 8 6 4 2
♢ J 10 6
♣ A

The bidding:

South	West	North	East
1 ♡	2 ♣	2 ♢	2 ♠
2 NT	Pass	3 NT	

Aramis opened with the ♣ 10. Winning with the ♣ A d'Artagnan realised that 4 ♡ would have been a much easier contract, but the play of 3 No Trumps became more amusing. So he led the ♡ 2 to the king and the ♡ 10 which he took over with the ♡ J. Athos who had followed with the ♣ J to the first trick now discarded the ♣ K, whereupon Aramis ducked once more hoping that d'Artagnan needed the heart suit so that Athos could also unblock the ♣ Q on the ♡ A! But d'Artagnan had smelled a rat. He was satisfied with the two heart tricks already won, working out that four diamond tricks and two spade tricks would bring the contract home. So he led the ♢ J and continued with the ♢ 10—but Athos ducked them both.

By now Athos and d'Artagnan could read each other's hands as if they were an open book. Athos tried to block dummy's diamonds and thus reduce the diamond tricks to three, but d'Artagnan's cards were the best and he knew how to use them so that Athos' fine defence was of no avail. After the second diamond trick d'Artagnan played three rounds of spades. Athos was able to take three spade tricks and the ♣ Q, but then had to give dummy the two missing diamond tricks.

After changing partners Athos once again demonstrated his confidence in d'Artagnan's ability by raising him to game on absolute rubbish.

South/Love all.

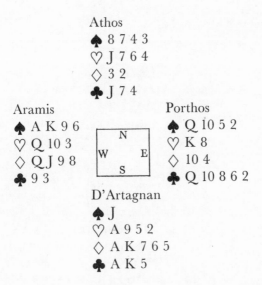

Athos
♠ 8 7 4 3
♡ J 7 6 4
◇ 3 2
♣ J 7 4

Aramis
♠ A K 9 6
♡ Q 10 3
◇ Q J 9 8
♣ 9 3

Porthos
♠ Q 10 5 2
♡ K 8
◇ 10 4
♣ Q 10 8 6 2

D'Artagnan
♠ J
♡ A 9 5 2
◇ A K 7 6 5
♣ A K 5

The bidding:

South	West	North	East
1 ◇	1 ♠	Pass	2 ♠
3 ♡	Pass	4 ♡	

Aramis led the two top spades and d'Artagnan ruffed the second. He then cashed two diamonds and ruffed the ◊ 5 with dummy's ♡ 4, which Porthos overruffed with the ♡ 8 in order to continue in spades. This was just what d'Artagnan wanted. He ruffed with the ♡ 5, drew the ♡ A, ruffed the ◊ 6 with dummy's ♡ 6, and then ruffed dummy's last spade with his own last trump. Following that he cashed the ♣ A and K and when he finally led the ◊ 7 Aramis could not stop dummy from winning the one trick with the ♡ J. This endplay is what we call nowadays 'Le Coup en passant'.

The following three deals were played during stays in Saint-Germain at 'Le Mouton-Courronné', in Neufchatel at 'La Herse d'Or' and in Compiègne at 'Le Paon-Courronné'.

South/Love all.

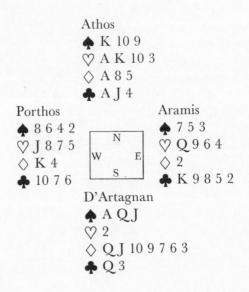

Athos
♠ K 10 9
♡ A K 10 3
◊ A 8 5
♣ A J 4

Porthos
♠ 8 6 4 2
♡ J 8 7 5
◊ K 4
♣ 10 7 6

Aramis
♠ 7 5 3
♡ Q 9 6 4
◊ 2
♣ K 9 8 5 2

D'Artagnan
♠ A Q J
♡ 2
◊ Q J 10 9 7 6 3
♣ Q 3

The bidding:	South	North
	1 ◊	7 ◊

Porthos opened with the ♣ 7 which d'Artagnan took with dummy's ace, whereupon he cashed the ♡ A–K and threw the ♣ Q. To try to learn where the ◇ K lay he quickly led the ♣ 4 from dummy, his hope being that Porthos' lead had been the next highest and that he therefore held the ♣ 10. By leading as he did he would make Aramis do a bit of thinking. Aramis was well aware of d'Artagnan's shrewdness, and that this would be the way he would play if he held the ♣ 10. Without the ◇ K he could only believe that the diamond suit was solid, and that the ♣ K might be the only chance to win a trick. If, on the other hand, he held the ◇ K (singleton or guarded) he could go up on the ♣ K without hesitating for a moment, particularly as with a ◇ K singleton he would quickly show the ♣ K so as to induce d'Artagnan to reckon with the other king with Porthos.

So, as d'Artagnan led the ♣ 4, and, moreover, as the previous tricks had been played very quickly, Aramis waited for a moment or two before going up with the ♣ K, but this was enough to convince d'Artagnan that Aramis was not holding the ◇ K, so he ruffed and led the ◇ Q, Porthos following with the ◇ 4. This was another hint, for supposing Porthos to be honest by playing his lowest diamond, Aramis would be holding the ◇ 2 and could not, therefore, hold the blank king. There was obviously every reason to finesse—and the grand slam was made.

D'Artagnan gave no reason for what he did, and when Porthos and Aramis grieved over his usual good luck in guessing correctly d'Artagnan simply said that he played on the equal possibility of the two missing kings being split.

South/Both.

D'Artagnan
♠ J 9 6 5
♡ Q J 5
◇ K 6 4
♣ J 9 7

Athos
♠ Q 2
♡ 10 8 6
◇ A Q J 8 7 5
♣ Q 2

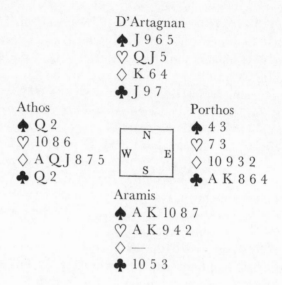

Porthos
♠ 4 3
♡ 7 3
◇ 10 9 3 2
♣ A K 8 6 4

Aramis
♠ A K 10 8 7
♡ A K 9 4 2
◇ —
♣ 10 5 3

The bidding:

South	West	North	East
1 ♠	2 ◇	2 ♠	3 ♣
3 ♡	Pass	4 ♠	

Athos led the ♣ Q and continued with the ♣ 2, Porthos cashing two more club tricks. When Aramis followed to three rounds of clubs, and had bid both the majors, Athos strongly suspected that he was void in diamonds, and the question now was how to stop Porthos from shifting to diamonds. And as the ◇ K fortunately was in dummy Athos could achieve this by jettisoning the ◇ A on the third club. Porthos was more than a little surprised by this discard, but it was quite plain that he should not lead a diamond. He understood Athos' intention and so played a fourth club with the consequence that Athos could not help but get the setting trick with the ♠ Q.

West/Both.

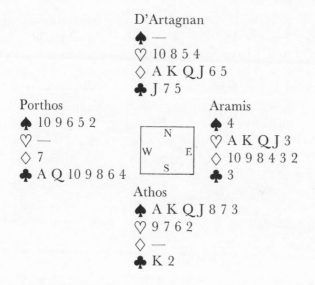

D'Artagnan
♠ —
♡ 10 8 5 4
♢ A K Q J 6 5
♣ J 7 5

Porthos
♠ 10 9 6 5 2
♡ —
♢ 7
♣ A Q 10 9 8 6 4

Aramis
♠ 4
♡ A K Q J 3
♢ 10 9 8 4 3 2
♣ 3

Athos
♠ A K Q J 8 7 3
♡ 9 7 6 2
♢ —
♣ K 2

The bidding:

West	North	East	South
Pass	Pass	1 ♡	1 ♠
3 ♣	3 ♢	Pass	4 ♠
Dble.	Pass	Pass	Redble.

Porthos laid down the ♣ A, and Athos quickly throwing his ♣ K completely confused Porthos who shifted to the ♢ 7. From this Athos understandingly concluded that Porthos was void in hearts, since Aramis without other values must hold a five-card-suit to open the bidding. Athos consequently ducked the diamond in dummy and ruffed with the ♠ 7. He then cashed the four highest trumps. Porthos was at least bright enough to know that it would be fatal to be endplayed in trumps and so he unblocked his four highest trumps. When Athos continued with the ♠ 3 Porthos was greatly amused when he ducked with the ♠ 2; but he nearly burst a blood vessel when Athos then laid down the ♣ 2. Porthos had to win the trick with the ♣ Q so as to limit Athos to one over-trick instead of two.

In 1950 one of Planchet's descendants informed the bridge world of two hands he had played following a method he had never seen described in any book, and which he called 'The Leska Coup'. The idea was to secure an extra trick by ruffing a top card with *the master trump*! Ten years later he found among Planchet's notes that d'Artagnan had originated this method more than three hundred years earlier. It could therefore, be well named as 'Le Coup de d'Artagnan'.

The game was being played one eveing in the inn 'Le Muid d'Amour' in the rue des Bourdonnais, and these were the four hands:

South/Love all.

Athos
♠ A J 9
♡ 9 8
◇ A Q 9
♣ K 9 7 6 4

Porthos
♠ K 10 8 7 3 2
♡ A K Q
◇ —
♣ Q 8 5 3

Aramis
♠ Q 6 5
♡ 7 3 2
◇ J 7 5 3
♣ A J 10

D'Artagnan
♠ 4
♡ J 10 6 5 4
◇ K 10 8 6 4 2
♣ 2

The bidding:

South	West	North	East
Pass	1 ♠	2 ♣	2 ♠
3 ◇	3 ♠	4 ◇	Dble.

Porthos led the ♡ K and then shifted to the ♣ Q which also held the trick. He continued with the ♣ 3, covered with the king and ace and ruffed with the ◇ 2. D'Artagnan led the ♠ 4 to the ace, ruffed the ♠ 9 with the ◇ 4 and then led the ♡ 5. Porthos won with the ♡ Q and led the ♠ K which d'Artagnan ruffed with the ◇ 6. D'Artagnan made the last six tricks by cross-ruffing clubs and hearts, while Aramis had to underruff four times without winning a trick. But as there were two top hearts which were ruffed with master trumps in the short trump hand this method should, properly, be called 'Le Double Coup de d'Artagnan'.

The next hand was dealt when the four men were playing in the 'Renard-Vert' in the rue du Vieux-Colombier!

North/E–W.

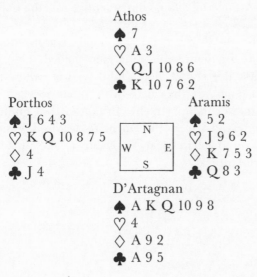

Athos
♠ 7
♡ A 3
◇ Q J 10 8 6
♣ K 10 7 6 2

Porthos
♠ J 6 4 3
♡ K Q 10 8 7 5
◇ 4
♣ J 4

Aramis
♠ 5 2
♡ J 9 6 2
◇ K 7 5 3
♣ Q 8 3

D'Artagnan
♠ A K Q 10 9 8
♡ 4
◇ A 9 2
♣ A 9 5

The bidding:

	North	South
	1 ◇	2 ♠
	3 ♣	4 NT
	5 ◇	5 NT
	6 ◇	6 ♠

Porthos led the ♡ K, taken with dummy's ace. Without appearing to show his disappointment with dummy's poor values d'Artagnan led the ◇ Q from dummy continuing with the ◇ 6 to the ◇ 9. Porthos ruffed and then continued hearts. D'Artagnan ruffed and cashed four high trumps and the ◇ A, discarding three clubs from dummy. When d'Artagnan cashed his last trump Aramis had to throw a club so as to keep the high diamond, and d'Artagnan had three club tricks.

In so far as d'Artagnan's abilities were concerned it was an easy hand, and it took him no more than thirty seconds to play it. The essential thing to do was to finesse diamonds immediately—if this was not done until the trumps had been drawn, then Aramis must hold the ◇ K doubleton. If the finesse should fail there must be no trump loser—but there was, and d'Artagnan's plan, consequently, was the one that led to success.

In the rue de Bussy stood the hotel 'L'Epée du Fier Cavalier' and frequently the four men played there. This hotel, in case the reader doesn't know, was where King Henri III's guards, 'the forty-five', often foregathered; further, in one of its apartments Ernauton de Comminges used to meet clandestinely the Duchesse de Montpensier.

And it was in this hotel that Athos showed the advantages of the surprise attack.

South/E–W.

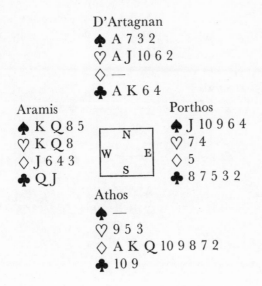

D'Artagnan
♠ A 7 3 2
♡ A J 10 6 2
◇ —
♣ A K 6 4

Aramis
♠ K Q 8 5
♡ K Q 8
◇ J 6 4 3
♣ Q J

Porthos
♠ J 10 9 6 4
♡ 7 4
◇ 5
♣ 8 7 5 3 2

Athos
♠ —
♡ 9 5 3
◇ A K Q 10 9 8 7 2
♣ 10 9

The bidding:

South	West	North	East
5 ◇	Pass	5 ♡	Pass
6 ◇	Dble.		

The ♠ K was led by Aramis, Athos ruffed with the ◇ 2 and without any hesitation played the ◇ 7! Aramis writhed as if he were in pain and came to the conclusion that Athos was trying to find the ◇ A singleton. So he followed with the ◇ 3, but Porthos could not beat Athos' ◇ 7, and the surprise attack had succeeded. Then trumps were drawn, a trick in hearts was lost, and the contract was made.

South/E–W.

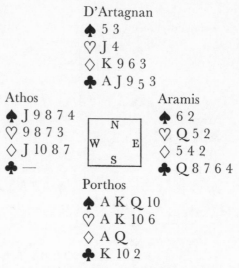

D'Artagnan
♠ 5 3
♡ J 4
◇ K 9 6 3
♣ A J 9 5 3

Athos
♠ J 9 8 7 4
♡ 9 8 7 3
◇ J 10 8 7
♣ —

Aramis
♠ 6 2
♡ Q 5 2
◇ 5 4 2
♣ Q 8 7 6 4

Porthos
♠ A K Q 10
♡ A K 10 6
◇ A Q
♣ K 10 2

The bidding:

South	North
3 NT	4 ♣
5 ♣	6 NT

Without being aware of it Porthos happened to squeeze Athos in this deal. Athos led the ♡ 9, covered with the jack and queen and won with the ♡ A. With the few entries in dummy Porthos had to cash the ♣ K, and seeing Athos void Porthos showed Aramis his cards saying:

'You should have the ♣ Q and I take the rest.'

But Aramis insisted that the hand should be played out, so Porthos continued with the ♣ 10 which Aramis let him hold. In the meantime Athos had run into difficulties—he had thrown a spade on the ♣ K and on the ♣ 10 he could spare nothing. Holding so many spades himself he was hoping that Porthos was short in this suit, so he discarded one more spade. Porthos then cashed two diamonds, entered dummy on the ♣ A, threw the ♡ 6 on the ◇ K, and took all thirteen tricks saying with a grumble:

'Well, it's up to you if you don't want to take any tricks.'

Sometimes d'Artagnan had the impression that Athos was too generous, but Porthos found this perfectly understandable in a peer of France who was wearing the uniform of the King's Musketeers. Even when playing cards Athos would often give a trick away, but when he did this one could be fairly certain that he hoped to be rewarded by getting two tricks back! In the next deal he was a spendthrift with the high cards, but even so that proved to be the only way to make the hand.

South/N–S.

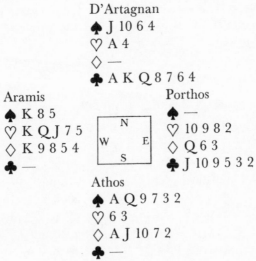

D'Artagnan
♠ J 10 6 4
♡ A 4
◇ —
♣ A K Q 8 7 6 4

Aramis
♠ K 8 5
♡ K Q J 7 5
◇ K 9 8 5 4
♣ —

Porthos
♠ —
♡ 10 9 8 2
◇ Q 6 3
♣ J 10 9 5 3 2

Athos
♠ A Q 9 7 3 2
♡ 6 3
◇ A J 10 7 2
♣ —

The bidding:

South	West	North	East
1 ♠	Dble.	Redble.	2 ♣
2 ◇	2 ♡	3 ♠	Pass
4 NT	Pass	5 ♡	Pass
6 ♠			

Aramis opened with the ♡ K, and dummy's ace won.

Athos was aware that there was a goulash distribution, and therefore he entered the closed hand by ruffing the ♣ 4 with the ♠ A so as to get rid of dummy's last heart on the ◇ A. He then led the ♠ 2 which was taken by Aramis with the king. Aramis now led the ♡ Q, which dummy ruffed with the ♠ 6. Athos then ruffed the ♣ 6 with the ♠ Q, entered dummy with the ♠ 3 to the ♠ 10 and ruffed dummy's ♣ 7 with the ♠ 9. Finally he played the ♠ 7 to dummy's ♠ J, at the same time drawing Aramis' last trump. Dummy's clubs were now high and they took the last four tricks.

The three musketeers had leave due to them and they decided to go to Boulogne, d'Artagnan joining them there at the hotel 'L'Epée du Grand Henri'. They might just as well have never left Paris for they spent the whole of the time playing bridge.

South/Both.

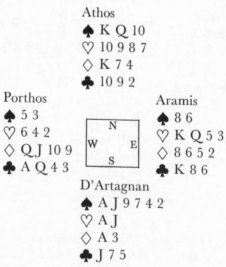

Athos
♠ K Q 10
♡ 10 9 8 7
◇ K 7 4
♣ 10 9 2

Porthos
♠ 5 3
♡ 6 4 2
◇ Q J 10 9
♣ A Q 4 3

Aramis
♠ 8 6
♡ K Q 5 3
◇ 8 6 5 2
♣ K 8 6

D'Artagnan
♠ A J 9 7 4 2
♡ A J
◇ A 3
♣ J 7 5

The bidding:

South	North
1 ♠	2 ♠
4 ♠	

Porthos led the ◇ Q and d'Artagnan played the ◇ 4 from dummy and the ◇ 3 from the closed hand! Even if Aramis had followed with the ◇ 2 Porthos could foresee no danger in continuing with the ◇ J. D'Artagnan won with the ◇ A and played the ♠ 2 to dummy's ♠ Q in order to lead the ♡ 10. Aramis covered with the ♡ Q. D'Artagnan won with the ♡ A entered dummy on the ♠ K, threw the ♡ J on the ◇ K, and then continued with the ♡ 9. Aramis' ♡ K was ruffed, the ♠ 10 was entry to dummy and d'Artagnan got rid of two of his losing clubs on the good hearts. So, instead of losing three clubs and one heart d'Artagnan lost only one diamond and one club, and made an overtrick.

North/Both.

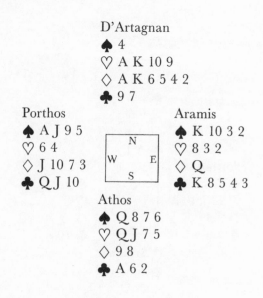

D'Artagnan
♠ 4
♡ A K 10 9
◇ A K 6 5 4 2
♣ 9 7

Porthos
♠ A J 9 5
♡ 6 4
◇ J 10 7 3
♣ Q J 10

Aramis
♠ K 10 3 2
♡ 8 3 2
◇ Q
♣ K 8 5 4 3

Athos
♠ Q 8 7 6
♡ Q J 7 5
◇ 9 8
♣ A 6 2

The bidding:

North	South
1 ◇	1 ♡
4 ♡	

Again Porthos led, this time the ♣ Q which Athos took with the ♣ A, after which he cashed the ♡ Q and played the ♡ 5 to dummy's king. Before drawing a third trump he sought to find the position of the diamonds by cashing the king. Aramis' following with the queen really meant nothing, but for safety's sake Athos continued with the ◇ 2 from dummy and literally gave Porthos a diamond trick. This, however, was absolutely necessary for the contract to be made. Porthos could now take a spade and a club, but the next black card was ruffed in dummy, a low diamond was ruffed with the ♡ J, and the ♡ 7 brought dummy on lead to the remaining tricks.

It can sometimes be embarrassing to hold too strong trumps by one defender, more especially so if it is disclosed to the declarer by a double.

North/Both.

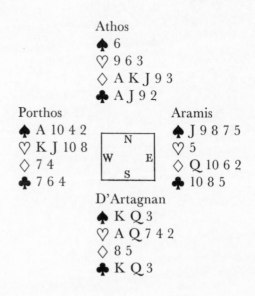

```
                        Athos
                        ♠ 6
                        ♡ 9 6 3
                        ◇ A K J 9 3
                        ♣ A J 9 2
        Porthos                         Aramis
        ♠ A 10 4 2          N           ♠ J 9 8 7 5
        ♡ K J 10 8      W       E       ♡ 5
        ◇ 7 4               S           ◇ Q 10 6 2
        ♣ 7 6 4                         ♣ 10 8 5
                        D'Artagnan
                        ♠ K Q 3
                        ♡ A Q 7 4 2
                        ◇ 8 5
                        ♣ K Q 3
```

The bidding:

North	East	South	West
1 ◇	Pass	1 ♡	Pass
2 ♡	Pass	3 NT	Pass
4 ♣	Pass	4 ♡	Dble.

When Porthos doubled d'Artagnan came to the conclusion that he must be holding strong trumps, for what else could he have? And it was on this supposition d'Artagnan based his play.

Porthos led the ♠ A and shifted to the ◇ 7 which was taken with dummy's king. After having cashed dummy's ♣ A d'Artagnan entered the closed hand on the ♣ K and cashed the ♠ K and Q, discarding dummy's two last clubs, and then the ♣ Q which Porthos had to follow, and a diamond to the ace. D'Artagnan now had seven tricks. A diamond was ruffed low and overruffed by Porthos who exited in spades. D'Artagnan then took his eighth trick with the ♡ 4 and led the ♡ 7. Porthos had to win with the ♡ 10 and to lead away from his ♡ K–J into declarer's tenace.

When the King's gift to d'Artagnan was finally spent the four friends simply could not afford to go out every night, but had to remain in their lodgings. One evening while the three musketeers were waiting for d'Artagnan in Athos' rooms in the rue Férou Aramis told the two other men about an interesting hand he had quite recently played in the home of a rather lovely lady, with whom he was friendly.

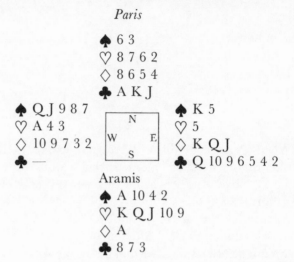

♠ 6 3
♡ 8 7 6 2
◇ 8 6 5 4
♣ A K J

♠ Q J 9 8 7
♡ A 4 3
◇ 10 9 7 3 2
♣ —

♠ K 5
♡ 5
◇ K Q J
♣ Q 10 9 6 5 4 2

Aramis
♠ A 10 4 2
♡ K Q J 10 9
◇ A
♣ 8 7 3

Aramis was playing in 4 ♡ as South. West was astute enough to open with the ♡ 3. Aramis won with the ♡ K, cashed the ♠ A and then led another spade. East was not clever enough to unblock the ♠ K and she had to win the trick. The lady had no trump to play and shifted to the ◇ K. Aramis was able to ruff two spades and easily scored ten tricks.

'But if East had unblocked the ♠ K?' Porthos asked.

'I make the contract anyway. West wins the second spade and naturally plays two rounds of trumps. I win, cash the ◇ A and then play a club to dummy's ace. I ruff a diamond in hand and a spade in dummy. Another diamond is led from dummy—and now East is allowed to hold the trick while I discard a spade. East has only clubs left and must, therefore, play into dummy's tenace.'

Athos was sceptical and said: 'You cannot make the contract against perfect defence. When West plays the ♡ A and the ♡ 4 East could unblock the ◇ K and the ◇ Q!'

'You think so!' Aramis exclaimed. 'Well then, when d'Artagnan arrives we will give him this hand and let him try to make the contract with that defence. I will play East and you, Porthos, play West.'

At that point d'Artagnan arrived, and greetings having been exchanged Aramis said:

'We have been waiting for you and you can see that the hands have already been dealt.'

D'Artagnan took his seat and picked up South's hand. He bid 1 ♡, Porthos 1 ♠, Aramis 3 ♣, d'Artagnan rebid 3 ♡, and Athos closed the auction with 4 ♡.

Porthos led the ♡ 3. D'Artagnan won, made a quick appraisal of the situation and led the ♣ 3! The three musketeers could scarcely conceal their surprise. Porthos threw a diamond seeing that there was nothing to be won by ruffing. D'Artagnan went up with dummy's king and played the ♠ 6 from dummy. Aramis followed with the ♠ 5. D'Artagnan won with the ace and continued with the ♠ 2 so that Aramis must win with the ♠ K. No defence could now set the contract.

The three musketeers were struck with amazement. D'Artagnan looked at them with surprise and said:

'You see, Aramis, that if you go up with the ♠ K you are allowed to hold the trick.'

It was not until later in the evening that Aramis owned up. D'Artagnan laughed and Athos simply commented:

'D'Artagnan , you are always resourceful.'

Aramis and Porthos had just won a rubber by one of the former's craftiest tricks. Athos changed places with Aramis while Porthos dealt the following cards:

North/Love all.

Porthos
♠ A K 5
♡ A K 5 2
◇ Q 10 7 4
♣ 5 3

Aramis
♠ 8
♡ J 9 8 7
◇ A K
♣ K Q J 8 6 2

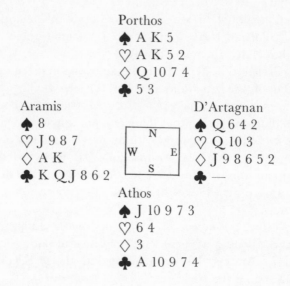

D'Artagnan
♠ Q 6 4 2
♡ Q 10 3
◇ J 9 8 6 5 2
♣ —

Athos
♠ J 10 9 7 3
♡ 6 4
◇ 3
♣ A 10 9 7 4

The bidding:

North	East	South	West
1 ♡	Pass	1 ♠	2 ♣
2 ♠	Pass	4 ♠	

Aramis opened with the ◇ A with the intention of following up with the ◇ K, but seeing dummy's cards he shifted to the ♣ K. D'Artagnan thought that the ◇ A had been a singleton and so he ruffed with the ♠ 4 to play a diamond. If Aramis could ruff, then the ♠ Q would give the setting trick. But it was Athos who ruffed—with the ♠ 9— and continued with the ♠ J—but he decided to go up with dummy's ♠ K and drew the ♠ A. And now d'Artagnan had to put on his thinking-cap. He had followed with the ♠ 6 to the first trump. It was easy for him to count Athos' distribution and he realised that if he followed with the ♠ 2 Athos would cash the ♡ A–K, ruff a heart and endplay him on the ♠ Q, thus compelling him to play diamonds into dummy's tenace at the same time as Aramis would be squeezed in hearts and clubs. So he unblocked the ♠ Q!

This ruined Athos' first plan, but he had another plan in reserve. He had lost only two tricks. He only needed to play the ♣ 5 from dummy. If d'Artagnan ruffed, then Athos could throw the ♣ 7, after which the ♠ 5 and the ◊ Q could take care of the remaining club losers. But if d'Artagnan did not ruff Athos could win with the ♣ A and ruff a club with the ♠ 5, which d'Artagnan could not overruff after the un-blockings—and even if he could he would have had to lead into the diamond tenace.

In this way the contract was cold, but rather maliciously Athos wondered whether he could put the thumbscrews on Aramis, just to repay his craftiness in the last deal. There was also the fact that, when he had the choice, Athos always preferred the most difficult plan. So for these reasons Athos played the ♠ 5 to the closed hand. Aramis threw the ♣ 6. There followed the ♡ A–K and the ◊ Q. Aramis could not afford to throw another club as Athos would then only need to lose a club to him; he threw a heart. But Athos ruffed a heart and had his three best clubs left against Aramis' ♣ Q–J–8. Athos led the ♣ 10, and Aramis won only one trick.

South/Both.

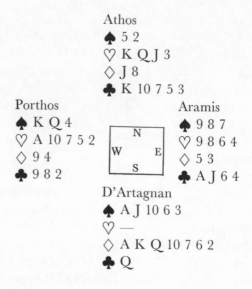

Athos
♠ 5 2
♡ K Q J 3
◇ J 8
♣ K 10 7 5 3

Porthos
♠ K Q 4
♡ A 10 7 5 2
◇ 9 4
♣ 9 8 2

Aramis
♠ 9 8 7
♡ 9 8 6 4
◇ 5 3
♣ A J 6 4

D'Artagnan
♠ A J 10 6 3
♡ —
◇ A K Q 10 7 6 2
♣ Q

The bidding:

South	West	North	East
1 ◇	1 ♡	2 ♣	Pass
2 ♠	Pass	3 NT	Pass
4 ♡	Pass	Pass!?	Pass

Athos' thoughts must have been miles away when he passed to 4 ♡. Porthos led the ♣ 9, and Aramis let it run to d'Artagnan's ♣ Q. D'Artagnan could only lead diamonds from top and hope for the best. Porthos ruffed the third diamond with the ♡ 5, and d'Artagnan threw dummy's ♠ 2. Somehow Porthos got the crazy idea that it must be important to remove dummy's trumps. and so he cashed the ♡ A and continued with the ♡ 2! Thankfully d'Artagnan drew the remaining trumps, entered his hand with the ♠ A and had the rest in diamonds. Five tricks were made in, of all things, hearts.

And so it came round for Porthos to be the host. His

apartment in the rue du Vieux-Colombier looked grand from the outside, but nobody had yet been inside for the very good reason that its vainglorious occupier dared not show how empty it was of furniture—for this particular occasion he had managed to borrow some.

South/Both.

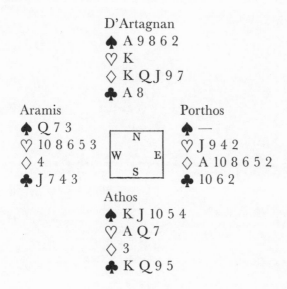

D'Artagnan
♠ A 9 8 6 2
♡ K
◇ K Q J 9 7
♣ A 8

Aramis
♠ Q 7 3
♡ 10 8 6 5 3
◇ 4
♣ J 7 4 3

Porthos
♠ —
♡ J 9 4 2
◇ A 10 8 6 5 2
♣ 10 6 2

Athos
♠ K J 10 5 4
♡ A Q 7
◇ 3
♣ K Q 9 5

The bidding:

South	North
1 ♠	2 ◇
3 ♣	4 NT
5 ◇	6 ♠

Aramis led the ◇ 4, and as Porthos had taken the ◇ J with the ace he led the ◇ 6 back. Athos went up with the ♠ K, his intention being to finesse spades through Aramis. But at the very moment as the ♠ K touched the table Aramis' ♠ 3 was there too: he was doing his level best to scrape home with the trick. He was stopped, of course, but Athos, who was only too well aware of Aramis' devious methods, was not in this particular case suspicious as it seemed to him to have happened without malice. Athos then played the ♠ J and Aramis followed with the ♠ 7. As the ♠ Q was now the only outstanding trump Athos decided after what had happened previsouly to play Porthos for the queen and went up with the ♠ A.

Thus there was another victory for the wily priest's pupil.

North/E–W.

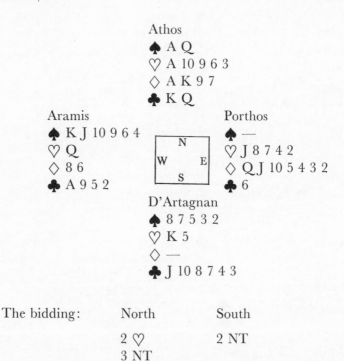

Athos
♠ A Q
♡ A 10 9 6 3
◇ A K 9 7
♣ K Q

Aramis
♠ K J 10 9 6 4
♡ Q
◇ 8 6
♣ A 9 5 2

Porthos
♠ —
♡ J 8 7 4 2
◇ Q J 10 5 4 3 2
♣ 6

D'Artagnan
♠ 8 7 5 3 2
♡ K 5
◇ —
♣ J 10 8 7 4 3

The bidding:	North	South
	2 ♡	2 NT
	3 NT	

Aramis opened with the ♠ J which was taken with the dummy's queen, and the ♣ K and Q were cashed as Aramis, of course, ducked and blocked the suit. In the meantime d'Artagnan had concluded that Porthos had a void in spades and a singleton club, with Aramis holding ten black cards. D'Artagnan cashed the two red aces in dummy to find out whether Aramis was void in one of these suits. Since this was not the case he also cashed the ♢ K and played a heart to the king so as to lay down the ♣ J, on which he unblocked dummy's ♠ A.

If Aramis were now to take his three spade tricks he must promote declarer's fifth spade. So he exited in clubs. It was, however, of no avail. D'Artagnan, who had discarded two clubs on the diamonds to keep all his spades intact, secured a spade trick by leading the ♠ 8 himself.

On the occasion when Aramis invited his friends to his elegant, if rather over-furnished, apartment there were no women present. This apartment was in the fashionable rue de Vaugirard. One of the first deals was as follows:

South/Love all.

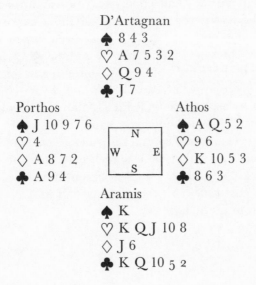

D'Artagnan
♠ 8 4 3
♡ A 7 5 3 2
♢ Q 9 4
♣ J 7

Porthos
♠ J 10 9 7 6
♡ 4
♢ A 8 7 2
♣ A 9 4

Athos
♠ A Q 5 2
♡ 9 6
♢ K 10 5 3
♣ 8 6 3

Aramis
♠ K
♡ K Q J 10 8
♢ J 6
♣ K Q 10 5 2

Paris

The bidding:

South	West	North	East
1 ♡	1 ♠	2 ♡	2 ♠
4 ♡			

Porthos led the ♠ J which Athos took with the ace and then shifted to the ◇ 3. Aramis covered with the ◇ J which Porthos, in turn, took with the ace, shifting back to the ♠ 10. Aramis ruffed and played the ♡ Q. He looked suspiciously at Porthos, thought for a short time, and finally went up on the ♡ A. He seemed to be disappointed when Athos followed with the ♡ 6. The ♣ J was now played from dummy, and Aramis, seemingly in difficulties, thought again before he decided to go up with the ♣ K.

Although Porthos had often been the victim of Aramis' trickery he had never experienced anything like this. For, when winning with the ♣ A he had been duped into the belief that Athos held both the ♡ K and the ♣ Q, and that consequently he risked nothing by continuing in spades. But this was precisely what Aramis had aimed at. He ruffed, drew Athos' last trump, and threw dummy's two diamonds on the good clubs in the closed hand. Athos could win no diamond trick and the contract was made.

It is well-known that while speech may be silver, silence, at times, can be gold; Aramis learned this in the next deal in which he could have set the contract had he not wakened Porthos from his dreams.

South/Love all.

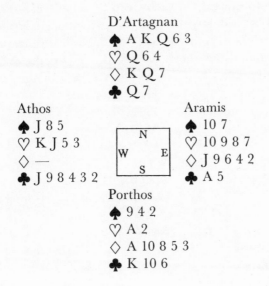

D'Artagnan
♠ A K Q 6 3
♡ Q 6 4
◇ K Q 7
♣ Q 7

Athos
♠ J 8 5
♡ K J 5 3
◇ —
♣ J 9 8 4 3 2

Aramis
♠ 10 7
♡ 10 9 8 7
◇ J 9 6 4 2
♣ A 5

Porthos
♠ 9 4 2
♡ A 2
◇ A 10 8 5 3
♣ K 10 6

The bidding:

	South	North
	1 ◇	2 NT
	3 ◇	4 NT
	5 ♡	6 ◇

Athos opened with the ♣ 4. Aramis won with the ♣ A and then shifted to the ♡ 10. Hesitating briefly Porthos went up with the ace, played the ♠ 9 to dummy's queen, and continued with the ♠ A and K. Aramis, believing that Porthos was now void in spades, threw the ♣ 5. The next spade Aramis ducked also, but when Porthos persisted with the fifth spade Aramis burst out:

'No, I ruff now!' And he did so with the ◇ 2.

'I'm sorry, but surely I'm playing 6 No Trumps?' Porthos interjected.

Aramis was very angry with himself for not having kept silent. Porthos, now fully awake, overruffed, played the ◇ 5 to dummy's queen, cashed the ◇ K, finessed in diamonds—

and drew the last trump. Athos, holding on to the ♡ K, had therefore to discard clubs down to the blank jack. Porthos, who had noticed only the dropping of a lot of clubs, took the last two tricks with the ♣ K–10. If Athos had discarded the ♡ K Porthos would surely have known to play the ♣ 10 and allowed dummy's two queens to take care of the last two tricks.

West/N–S.

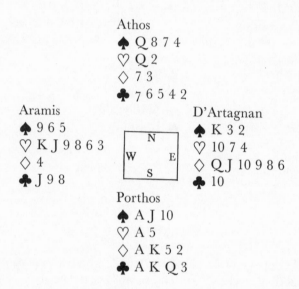

Athos
♠ Q 8 7 4
♡ Q 2
◇ 7 3
♣ 7 6 5 4 2

Aramis
♠ 9 6 5
♡ K J 9 8 6 3
◇ 4
♣ J 9 8

D'Artagnan
♠ K 3 2
♡ 10 7 4
◇ Q J 10 9 8 6
♣ 10

Porthos
♠ A J 10
♡ A 5
◇ A K 5 2
♣ A K Q 3

After two passes d'Artagnan shrewdly opened with 1 ◇. Porthos doubled. Aramis bid 1 ♡, and Athos incautiously bid 1 ♠, even though his hand was not worth a bid. But Porthos had just misplayed a pair of ice-cold contracts, and if spades were his strength Athos would try to become the declarer. But Porthos was certain in his own mind that East–West were bluffing, and so he went directly into 6 No Trumps.

The ◇ 4 was led and Porthos won with the ◇ K. He cashed five club tricks and on the fifth he intended to throw the ♡ 5, but he pulled the wrong card and the ♡ A lay on the table. He picked it up under strong protests from Aramis. Athos sensibly said that Aramis was within his rights, but consoled Porthos by saying that it didn't matter all that much. Reluctantly Porthos left the ♡ A lying. He continued with the ♠ Q from dummy which d'Artagnan covered with the king, and Porthos cashed all his certain tricks.

But if Porthos had now been holding the ♡ A as one of his last three cards he would have had to lose two diamond tricks. So he was left with the ♡ 5 which he duly led. And what a difference! Aramis could take only the ♡ K and thus had to give dummy the ♡ Q and the thirteenth spade.

With Aramis sticking strictly to the rules Porthos was able to make the slam.

North/N–S.

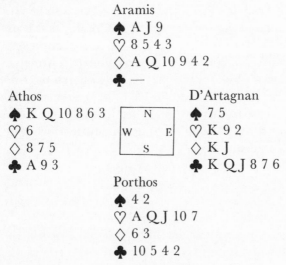

Aramis
♠ A J 9
♡ 8 5 4 3
◇ A Q 10 9 4 2
♣ —

Athos
♠ K Q 10 8 6 3
♡ 6
◇ 8 7 5
♣ A 9 3

D'Artagnan
♠ 7 5
♡ K 9 2
◇ K J
♣ K Q J 8 7 6

Porthos
♠ 4 2
♡ A Q J 10 7
◇ 6 3
♣ 10 5 4 2

The bidding:

North	East	South	West
1 ◇	2 ♣	2 ♡	2 ♠
4 ♡	Pass	Pass	4 ♠
5 ♡	Dble.		

Athos led the ♣ A which was ruffed with dummy's ♡ 3. Porthos led the ♡ 4 to the queen and thoughtfully looked at his diamond suit while dummy still had trumps to stop the clubs. So he played the ◇ 6 to the queen—and d'Artagnan followed with the ◇ J! The position being as it was with both the trumps and the diamonds(?) duly located, Porthos played the ♡ 5 to the jack and then laid down the ♡ A. Following which he played the ◇ 3 to dummy's ◇ 9. But d'Artagnan now took the trick with his blank king and then cashed three club tricks. That made it two down!

On the following day d'Artganan was visited by his landlord, the grocer Bonacieux. Bonacieux asked for his, and his friends', help in connection with the kidnapping of his wife. A little later on d'Artagnan asked his friends to repeat their visit as his landlord had given him several bottles of their favourite Anjou wine in the hope of services to be rendered. They were all in excellent spirits as a result, that is until the Cardinal's guards arrived on the scene to arrest poor Bonacieux. To Porthos' great resentment d'Artagnan paid no attention as this was done; he even offered the Captain a drink and fooled him and his fellow guards by drinking with them a toast to the Cardinal's health. Without any further explanations to Porthos d'Artagnan cut the cards and asked Porthos to deal.

South/Love all.

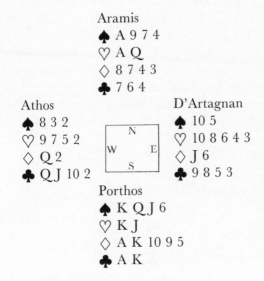

Aramis
♠ A 9 7 4
♡ A Q
♢ 8 7 4 3
♣ 7 6 4

Athos
♠ 8 3 2
♡ 9 7 5 2
♢ Q 2
♣ Q J 10 2

D'Artagnan
♠ 10 5
♡ 10 8 6 4 3
♢ J 6
♣ 9 8 5 3

Porthos
♠ K Q J 6
♡ K J
♢ A K 10 9 5
♣ A K

At the start d'Artagnan and Athos took no part in the bidding:

South	North
2 ♢	3 NT
4 ♢	6 ♢
7 ♢	Pass

At this point d'Artagnan came to life with a double. His hand was certainly not worth a single trick, but what could happen? Overtricks were in any case excluded. But perhaps Athos could take a trick, particularly if Porthos, through the double, could get a wrong impression as to who might hold an eventual key card.

Athos led the ♣ Q. Porthos won and played the ♡ J to the queen in order to play a trump from dummy. D'Artagnan bluffed again by playing the ♢ J. Porthos scowled at him and entered dummy on the ♡ A to play another trump. For very good reasons d'Artagnan could only play the ♢ 6, but

Porthos thought it a certainty that d'Artagnan also held the ◇ Q, for what else could his double have been made on? With a loud chuckle he finessed with the ◇ 9, thinking up a sarcastic remark about idiotic doubles of slam contracts. When Athos took the trick with the ◇ Q, and the cold slam went down, the sarcasm changed into full-blooded oaths.

As has been shown before Athos never followed any beaten track—it was in his nature always to prefer the unorthodox and more difficult way, as can be shown from this deal:

East/Both.

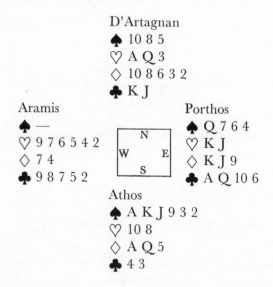

D'Artagnan
♠ 10 8 5
♡ A Q 3
◇ 10 8 6 3 2
♣ K J

Aramis
♠ —
♡ 9 7 6 5 4 2
◇ 7 4
♣ 9 8 7 5 2

Porthos
♠ Q 7 6 4
♡ K J
◇ K J 9
♣ A Q 10 6

Athos
♠ A K J 9 3 2
♡ 10 8
◇ A Q 5
♣ 4 3

The bidding:

East	South	West	North
1 NT	2 ♠	Pass	4 ♠

Aramis opened with the ♣ 9. After two club tricks Porthos continued with the ♣ 10. At this point Athos might have discarded the ◇ 5 and ruffed in dummy so as to lead the the ♠ 10. But this was a too simple thing for him to do.

Instead he ruffed in the closed hand with the ♠ 3 and over-ruffed with dummy's ♠ 5, then playing the ◇ 2 to the queen, cashing the ◇ A and playing the ◇ 5 to Porthos' king. Porthos persisted with his last club, and again Athos might have thrown a heart and ruffed in dummy to play the ♠ 10, shorten his trump length on a diamond and enter dummy again on the ♡ A.

However, Athos preferred to ruff with the ♠ 2 and over-ruff with dummy's ♠ 8. He then led the ♠ 10, which Porthos had to duck, and dummy's high diamonds followed. Porthos' trumps were taken with ease and Athos made his contract by double underruffing and double trump reduction.

South/Love all.

Aramis
♠ A J 10 8
♡ Q J 8
◇ J 4
♣ Q 10 8 5

D'Artagnan
♠ 9
♡ 10 5 4 2
◇ A Q 9 7 5
♣ A K 2

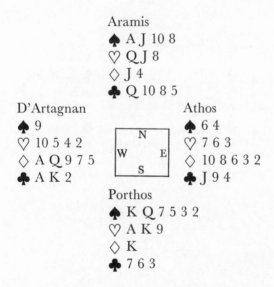

Athos
♠ 6 4
♡ 7 6 3
◇ 10 8 6 3 2
♣ J 9 4

Porthos
♠ K Q 7 5 3 2
♡ A K 9
◇ K
♣ 7 6 3

The bidding:

South	West	North	East
1 ♠	2 ◇	2 ♠	Pass
4 ♠			

D'Artagnan led the ♣ A and from this Athos well understood that something out of the usual would have to be done to set the contract. He consequently played the ♣ 9. D'Artagnan continued with the ♣ K, and when Athos followed with the ♣ 4 everyone believed that he originally held a doubleton and was now void. When d'Artagnan continued with the ♣ 2 Porthos, of course, finessed with the ♣ 10. Athos won the trick with the ♣ J and then shifted to diamonds—and the contract went one down.

South/Both.

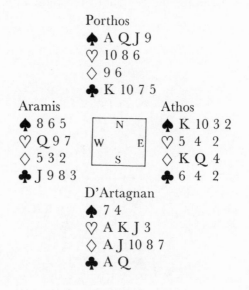

Porthos
♠ A Q J 9
♡ 10 8 6
♢ 9 6
♣ K 10 7 5

Aramis
♠ 8 6 5
♡ Q 9 7
♢ 5 3 2
♣ J 9 8 3

Athos
♠ K 10 3 2
♡ 5 4 2
♢ K Q 4
♣ 6 4 2

D'Artagnan
♠ 7 4
♡ A K J 3
♢ A J 10 8 7
♣ A Q

The bidding:	South	North
	1 ♢	1 ♠
	2 NT	3 NT

Aramis led the ♣ 3 which d'Artagnan took with the ♣ Q to lead the ♠ 7 to the ♠ J. Athos ducked so as to tempt d'Artagnan into finessing again and thus break the connexion with dummy. Now the ♢ 9 was led from dummy. Athos

split his honours and d'Artagnan won with the ace and
continued with the ◇ J. Athos won and shifted to the ♡ 2.
D'Artagnan won with the ♡ A, cashed the ♣ A and three
good diamonds, and played the ♠ 4 to dummy's ace. From
dummy he had thrown two spades and a heart to the
diamonds, feeling that Athos held the ♠ K, but had ducked
as he would have done himself had he been East. Aramis
had thrown two spades and now had to discard a heart to
save the clubs. After having cashed dummy's ♣ K d'Artagnan therefore led a heart to the king and took the rest of the
tricks—twelve in all.

THE 'MOUSETRAP'

After their arrest of Bonacieux the Cardinal's guards set a
trap in his shop and private apartments, for Constance had
successfully evaded capture. She was a good-looking young
woman, a niece of one of the Queen's servants named
Laporte who had been able to get her a position in the
Queen's service.

Without going into too much detail she had become
involved in a court intrigue and as a result offended Cardinal
Richelieu. She walked into the trap when she came to see her
husband, and by freeing her d'Artagnan automatically
became involved in the whole affair. When, later on, he
escorted Constance and the Duke of Buckingham (who was
disguised as a musketeer) back to the Louvre it was too
dangerous for him to return to the rue des Fosseyeurs where
Athos, meanwhile, had allowed himself to be arrested so that
d'Artagnan could have a free hand in his actions.

D'Artagnan had, through the agency of Planchet, made
an appointment to meet Aramis and Porthos at the inn 'La
Pomme-de-Pin', and as far as d'Artagnan was concerned that
was the end of matters for the night. When he arrived at the
inn he found his two friends had with them a young musketeer, de Montaran, and while they waited to see how things
developed they played a rubber which in itself had some of
the drama of the evening's earlier events.

North/Both.

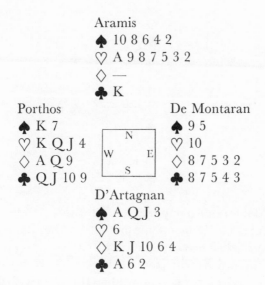

Aramis
♠ 10 8 6 4 2
♡ A 9 8 7 5 3 2
◊ —
♣ K

Porthos
♠ K 7
♡ K Q J 4
◊ A Q 9
♣ Q J 10 9

De Montaran
♠ 9 5
♡ 10
◊ 8 7 5 3 2
♣ 8 7 5 4 3

D'Artagnan
♠ A Q J 3
♡ 6
◊ K J 10 6 4
♣ A 6 2

The bidding:

North	East	South	West
Pass	Pass	1 ◊	1 NT
2 ♡	Pass	2 ♠	Pass
5 ♠	Pass	6 ♠	Dble.
Redble.			

Porthos became more and more confused as the bidding rose to extraordinary heights, and his double sounded like a thunderclap. He led the ♣ Q. Very quickly d'Artagnan cashed dummy's ♣ K and ♡ A and cross-ruffed hearts and diamonds until the following position was reached:

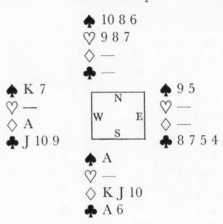

♠ 10 8 6
♡ 9 8 7
◇ —
♣ —

♠ K 7   ♠ 9 5
♡ —   ♡ —
◇ A   ◇ —
♣ J 10 9   ♣ 8 7 5 4

♠ A
♡ —
◇ K J 10
♣ A 6

De Montaran's many diamond discards had been rather unnerving, but it might mean that on the other hand he could probably overruff some of dummy's trumps so that Porthos was left with the doubleton ♠ K. D'Artagnan therefore cashed the ♠ A and ruffed the ◇ 10 with dummy's ♠ 10! Then he led the ♠ 8 from dummy, throwing the ♣ 6 from the closed hand. Porthos won the trick with the ♠ K, but this was his only trick; he had only clubs left and had to give d'Artagnan the last three tricks.

Through the intervention of de Tréville Athos was freed and, naturally, a celebration was indicated. Bottles of wine were procured and a rubber, without de Montaran, was played.

West/E–W.

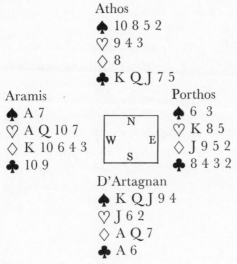

Athos
♠ 10 8 5 2
♡ 9 4 3
◇ 8
♣ K Q J 7 5

Aramis
♠ A 7
♡ A Q 10 7
◇ K 10 6 4 3
♣ 10 9

Porthos
♠ 6 3
♡ K 8 5
◇ J 9 5 2
♣ 8 4 3 2

D'Artagnan
♠ K Q J 9 4
♡ J 6 2
◇ A Q 7
♣ A 6

The bidding:

West	North	East	South
1 ♡	Pass	1 NT	3 ♠
Pass	4 ♠		

Aramis led the ♣ 10 and as the contract looked quite hopeless d'Artagnan had to think carefully before he followed with the ♣ 5 from dummy and won with the ♣ A. He was fully aware that, the clubs being disclosed, if a trump was played then Aramis would hasten to win and shift to hearts. Neither could he rely upon the clubs being 3–3 or that Aramis held only two clubs and the singleton ♠ A.

D'Artagnan had to consider all this in less time that it has taken to explain, but it was sufficient to give him a bright idea which, however, he would never have tried if Porthos had been West. He laid down the ◇ Q! As West Porthos would, without reflexion, have won with the king and cashed the ♡ A. But Aramis was far too astute. With a singleton diamond, and plenty of trumps, in dummy no one would dream that d'Artagnan held the ◇ A when he played the queen. Aramis felt that Porthos' 1 No Trump was based upon the ◇ A and that d'Artagnan held the ♡ K. It was most important, therefore, to get Porthos to play hearts through the declarer's king. After these considerations, which d'Artagnan knew Aramis was well able to take into account, Aramis ducked. It was then that d'Artagnan hastened to cash the ◇ A, to throw a heart from dummy and only then to lead the ♠ J. Aramis went up with the ♠ A and shifted to hearts; but it was too late to get more than two tricks in hearts—and d'Artagnan had made the hopeless contract.

In their rather festive mood nobody could be really angry with Aramis even at his worst behaviour.

West/E–W.

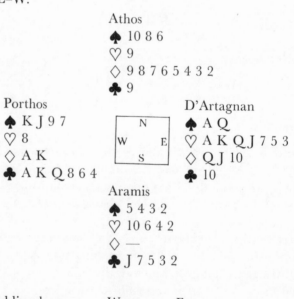

Athos
♠ 10 8 6
♡ 9
◇ 9 8 7 6 5 4 3 2
♣ 9

Porthos
♠ K J 9 7
♡ 8
◇ A K
♣ A K Q 8 6 4

D'Artagnan
♠ A Q
♡ A K Q J 7 5 3
◇ Q J 10
♣ 10

Aramis
♠ 5 4 3 2
♡ 10 6 4 2
◇ —
♣ J 7 5 3 2

The bidding began:

West	East
1 ♣	2 ♡
2 ♠	4 NT
5 ♡	5 NT
6 ♠	7 ♡

Porthos, getting excited by the high bidding, handed his cards to d'Artagnan and asked whether he could look at his. The exchange made Aramis coldly remarked:

'Wouldn't it be a good idea to finish the bidding?' And he thereupon bid 7 No Trumps which Porthos doubled and Aramis redoubled.

Porthos led his singleton ♡ 8.

'Now, just a minute,' Aramis said. 'You seem to have forgotten that those twenty-six cards of yours are 'exposed' cards, and that it is *me* who decides what to play and what to discard.'

Porthos and d'Artagnan had to put their cards on the table, and under Aramis' direction the hand was played in this most curious way: Aramis peremptorily asked for the ♣ 8 from West, won with the ♣ J, and continued with the ♣ 7 and the ♣ 5 which West had to duck with the ♣ 6 and the ♣ 4 whilst East was ordered to unblock the two high spades. There then followed the ♠ 2 to dummy's ♠ 10, drawing the ♠ 9 from West, followed again by the ♠ 8 ducked by West with the ♠ 7. Aramis then took three heart tricks which East had to duck. West had to unblock the two high spades and dummy the ♠ 6 so that Aramis could cash the ♠ 5 and the ♠ 4. On these West was told to throw the ♣ A and K. East, who had already unblocked the ♡ A and K on the spades, now got rid of the ♡ Q and J. After all this the ♡ 2 was high so that West could throw the ♣ Q, and then Aramis finally took the last two tricks with the ♣ 3 and 2. After this quite fantastic run of play, during which his opponents had to carry out double, triple and quadruple unblocking, Aramis had made his contract—7 No Trumps redoubled.

Aramis' apartment in the rue de Vaugirard has already been referred to, and with the elegance of its furniture was a fitting place to stay when the lovely Duchesse de Chevreuse made her secret visit to Paris in connexion with the plot involving the Duke of Buckingham. However, after she had left, Aramis could once again entertain his friends.

South/N–S.

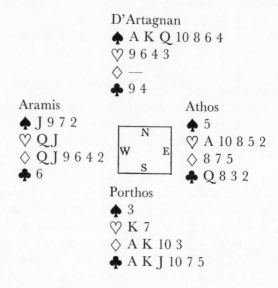

D'Artagnan
♠ A K Q 10 8 6 4
♡ 9 6 4 3
♢ —
♣ 9 4

Aramis
♠ J 9 7 2
♡ Q J
♢ Q J 9 6 4 2
♣ 6

Athos
♠ 5
♡ A 10 8 5 2
♢ 8 7 5
♣ Q 8 3 2

Porthos
♠ 3
♡ K 7
♢ A K 10 3
♣ A K J 10 7 5

The bidding:

South	West	North	East
1 ♣	1 ♢	1 ♠	Pass
2 NT	Pass	4 NT	Pass
5 ♡	Pass	6 ♠	Pass
6 NT			

Aramis led the ♡ Q. Athos went up with the ace and returned the ♡ 2 to Porthos' king. If Porthos had had full knowledge of 'safety' play he would possibly have cashed the ♣ A before trying out the spade suit, but it was fortunate that he didn't. He immediately played spades from the top, throwing two diamonds. Since the spades did not provide more than three tricks he had to resort to the clubs, and as it was clear that Aramis was short in these Porthos led dummy's ♣ 9 and let it run. He was lucky, and another club finesse brought him the rest of the tricks.

With the apparently successful outcome of the Bonacieux

affair the four men could once again fraternise in the rue des Fossoyeurs.

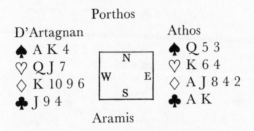

As East Athos ended in 6 No Trumps, and Aramis led the ♡ 10. Porthos won with the ace and then returned the ♡ 5 which Athos took with the king. Aramis let one of his cards fall on the floor and as he picked it up his hand, which included the lonely ◇ 7 on the one end, was shown 'accidently' to Athos. Athos now played the ◇ J to the king and the ◇ 10 back to the ace, and somewhat crestfallen Aramis had to follow with the ◇ Q.

'You should not let your cards be seen, Aramis,' Athos remarked.

'But I know that you wouldn't even glance at them, Athos.'

'When you almost hold your cards under my nose, how could I avoid seeing your blank .◇ 7?'

'In that case why on earth didn't you finesse?'

'For the very good and simple reason that I never take advantage of unasked for information,' Athos answered with a playful smile.

Athos' masterful play and his nonchalance in the jettisoning of high cards can be seen again in the following deal:

South/Both.

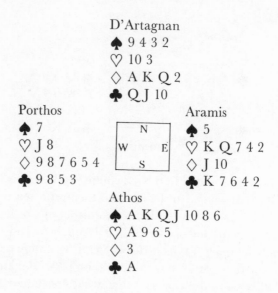

D'Artagnan
♠ 9 4 3 2
♡ 10 3
♦ A K Q 2
♣ Q J 10

Porthos
♠ 7
♡ J 8
♦ 9 8 7 6 5 4
♣ 9 8 5 3

Aramis
♠ 5
♡ K Q 7 4 2
♦ J 10
♣ K 7 6 4 2

Athos
♠ A K Q J 10 8 6
♡ A 9 6 5
♦ 3
♣ A

The bidding: South   North

                    2 ♠   3 NT
                    6 ♠   7 ♠

Porthos led his highest diamond, and Athos won with dummy' queen. He could count up to twelve certain tricks, but to get the thirteenth, to take care of his last heart, he had to find the ♣ K in Aramis' hand so that he could set up a club by ruffing. The diamond lead, however, removed one of dummy's entries, and as the trumps in the closed hand were blocking there was only one trump entry on the ♠ 9. That is, when the enemy's trumps and the ♣ A had been drawn then Athos could with certainty enter dummy on the ♠ 9, but he could *not* re-enter dummy if Aramis covered the ♣ Q. In his own inimitable way Athos solved the problem. He cashed another high diamond and jettisoned the ♣ A! Then he played the ♣ Q and ruffed Aramis' king with the ♠ A.

After having drawn the ♠ K he played the ♠ 6 to dummy's ♠ 9, and the last three low hearts were thrown on the two high clubs and the last high diamond.

THE DIAMOND STUDS

The dilemma that Queen Anne was in can well be imagined. Cardinal Richelieu had discovered that she had given the casket containing the twelve diamond studs, which was a present from the King, to the Duke of Buckingham. Constance Bonacieux, the little grocer's wife, suggested that her husband should travel to England to reclaim them, but as Dumas' afficionados well know, it was d'Artagnan and the three musketeers who were given that undertaking. While their servants were getting their baggage ready for the journey and looking after the horses there was some time to spare, time enough for a few rubbers.

South/Both.

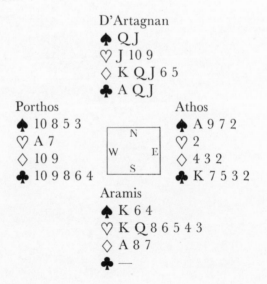

D'Artagnan
♠ Q J
♡ J 10 9
◇ K Q J 6 5
♣ A Q J

Porthos
♠ 10 8 5 3
♡ A 7
◇ 10 9
♣ 10 9 8 6 4

Athos
♠ A 9 7 2
♡ 2
◇ 4 3 2
♣ K 7 5 3 2

Aramis
♠ K 6 4
♡ K Q 8 6 5 4 3
◇ A 8 7
♣ —

The bidding:

	South	North
	1 ♡	2 ◇
	3 ♡	5 ♡
	6 ♡	

Porthos led the ♣ 10. Aramis was not at all happy to see that d'Artagnan was holding the wrong ace, but he tried to make things as difficult as he could for his opponents by going up with the dummy's ♣ A and throwing the ◇ 8 from the closed hand. He then continued with the ♣ Q which was covered by Athos. Aramis ruffed and played the ♡ 4. As Porthos saw it it looked as if Aramis was in a hurry to enter dummy so that he could throw another diamond on the ♣ J. So he went up with the ♡ A at once and then shifted to a diamond, and Aramis got rid of all his spades on dummy's diamonds.

Aramis' shrewd plan was a perfectly honest one, and it was conceived so as to continue in clubs. Had he played a trump immediately Porthos might, perhaps, have ducked a round, and would then have been given a spade echo from Athos.

On their way to England a halt was made at Chantilly to rest and water the horses; here it was that one of the Cardinal's men annoyed and provoked Porthos, believing him to be the head of the party because of his loud and commanding voice. While the horses were being watered the musketeers had found the time to play a few hands, and one of the hands dealt was the following:

South/Both.

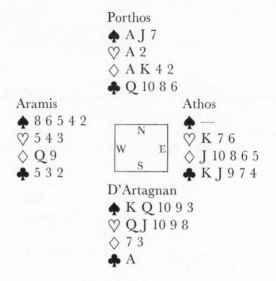

Porthos
♠ A J 7
♡ A 2
◇ A K 4 2
♣ Q 10 8 6

Aramis
♠ 8 6 5 4 2
♡ 5 4 3
◇ Q 9
♣ 5 3 2

Athos
♠ —
♡ K 7 6
◇ J 10 8 6 5
♣ K J 9 7 4

D'Artagnan
♠ K Q 10 9 3
♡ Q J 10 9 8
◇ 7 3
♣ A

The bidding:	South	North
	1 ♠	2 ◇
	2 ♡	3 ♠
	4 ♠	4 NT
	5 ◇	5 NT
	6 ◇	6 ♠

Aramis led the ♣ 5 which d'Artagnan took with his singleton ace. The ♠ 3 to dummy's ♠ J showed the bad trump
position. Hearts had now to be established before d'Artagnan
could continue in trumps, but d'Artagnan first cashed one of
dummy's diamond honours, then the ♡ A and the ♡ 2.
Athos won with the king and shifted to the most embarrassing
card for d'Artagnan—the ♣ K. He had to ruff and was now
one trump shorter than Aramis. But it didn't matter—
d'Artagnan played hearts and more hearts. If Aramis ruffed
dummy would overruff with the ♠ A, and all his trumps
could be drawn, so he didn't ruff. From dummy all three

diamonds were thrown, while Aramis first threw the ◇ Q
and then clubs. The last heart had been cashed, and
d'Artagnan ruffed the ◇ 7 with dummy's ♠ A, and took the
rest with top trumps, Aramis having to underruff the whole
time.

It should be mentioned here that Porthos was wounded at
Chantilly and was left there. The same thing happened to
Aramis at Crèvecoeur and to Athos at Amiens. No more
bridge! However, d'Artagnan succeeded in his commission,
the diamond studs were returned to the Queen in the nick of
time, and d'Artagnan was able to find out what had become
of his three friends. At Chantilly he found Porthos well on the
way to recovery, but at Crèvecoeur it was a very different
story—Aramis was infinitely depressed. He had no news from
his latest ladylove. Moreover, he was blessed with the company of the Prior of the Jesuits at Amiens and the priest from
Montdidier. It had always been Aramis' intention to rejoin
his clerical order, and in his present depressed mood he was
thinking about it very seriously. But when d'Artagnan gave
him the letter he had been expecting from his Paris address
his mood quickly changed. Rejecting the lenten meal that
had been prepared, and while a new and more lavish dinner
was being cooked, he even induced the two clerics to join in
a game of bridge.

South/E–W.

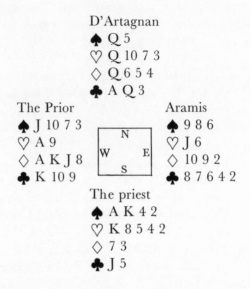

D'Artagnan
♠ Q 5
♡ Q 10 7 3
♦ Q 6 5 4
♣ A Q 3

The Prior
♠ J 10 7 3
♡ A 9
♦ A K J 8
♣ K 10 9

Aramis
♠ 9 8 6
♡ J 6
♦ 10 9 2
♣ 8 7 6 4 2

The priest
♠ A K 4 2
♡ K 8 5 4 2
♦ 7 3
♣ J 5

The bidding:

South	West	North	East
1 ♡	Dble.	Redble.	2 ♣
Pass	Pass	4 ♡	Pass
Pass	Dble.		

The Prior cashed two diamonds and shifted to the ♣ 10. The priest went up with dummy's ace, threw his last club on the ♦ Q and then played the ♡ 3 to the king. The Prior won with the ♡ A and played the ♣ K which the priest ruffed. At this point Aramis, the church's estimable pupil, gestured as if he would throw in his cards, saying:

'Is there any reason to play the hand out?'

This lack of good taste led the priest to finesse the ♡ 10 in the next trick, and Aramis took the undertrick with the bare ♡ J.

South/Love all.

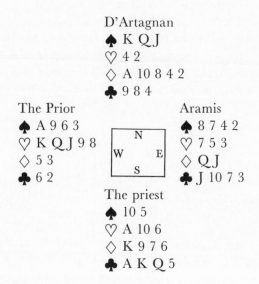

D'Artagnan
♠ K Q J
♡ 4 2
♢ A 10 8 4 2
♣ 9 8 4

The Prior
♠ A 9 6 3
♡ K Q J 9 8
♢ 5 3
♣ 6 2

Aramis
♠ 8 7 4 2
♡ 7 5 3
♢ Q J
♣ J 10 7 3

The priest
♠ 10 5
♡ A 10 6
♢ K 9 7 6
♣ A K Q 5

The bidding:

South	West	North	East
1 ♢	1 ♡	3 ♢	Pass
3 NT			

In this deal the Prior led the ♡ K which the priest took at once with his ace so that he could play three rounds of clubs. On the third round the Prior dropped the ♢ 3. Aramis could see that the contract was cold—but he then suddenly got an idea, and threw the ♠ 2.

'Have you no clubs?' the Prior and the priest asked in unison, much surprised.

'You must forgive me,' Aramis replied, taking up the Prior's ♢ 3! He could now stop the diamonds and the contract went three down—the Prior, naturally, sticking to the ♠ A and the four good hearts.

On the following day d'Artagnan inquired about Athos at the inn 'Le Lis d'Or' in Amiens to be told that Athos and his servant, Grimaud, had barricaded themselves in the wine cellar and were busy drinking as much as they could. D'Artagnan sorted matters out and after a well-spent night their famous game of dice was played on the following morning. History does not tell us, however, that Athos and d'Artagnan also played bridge with the two Englishmen, and that this hand was dealt:

South/N–S.

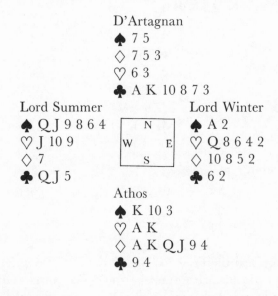

D'Artagnan
♠ 7 5
◇ 7 5 3
♡ 6 3
♣ A K 10 8 7 3

Lord Summer
♠ Q J 9 8 6 4
♡ J 10 9
◇ 7
♣ Q J 5

Lord Winter
♠ A 2
♡ Q 8 6 4 2
◇ 10 8 5 2
♣ 6 2

Athos
♠ K 10 3
♡ A K
◇ A K Q J 9 4
♣ 9 4

The bidding:

South	West	North	East
1 ◇	1 ♠	2 ♣	Pass
6 NT			

While the bidding was in progress Athos had to ask Lord Summer to hold his hand higher up; but while he was considering what to lead Lord Summer forgot what he had been asked and Athos could not help seeing his cards. This was embarrassing because no one had better manners than Athos. Lord Summer led the ♠ Q. Lord Winter went up with the ace and returned the ♠ 2, which Athos, naturally took with the king. After having cashed the ◇ A he played the ♣ 9, and when Lord Summer followed with the ♣ 5 Athos said:

'I couldn't help seeing your ♣ Q–J, but I am not going to take advantage of you.' He then went up with dummy's ace, and Lord Summer complimented him.

Nevertheless Athos easily made the slam. He cashed all his diamonds and hearts until only two cards were left. Lord Summer had to keep the ♣ Q–J, and could only hope that Lord Winter held the ♠ 10—which, as you see, he did not.

D'Artagnan had brought over from England four magnificent horses with their full equipment, but to his extreme annoyance Athos had gambled away two of the horses to the Englishmen. At Crèvecoeur they picked up Aramis and when all four were reunited at Chantilly it appeared that the other two musketeers had sold their horses but, oddly, had kept their saddles. D'Artagnan was good-natured enough to laugh at what they had done.

It probably goes without saying that their reunion was celebrated at the card-table, but not until they had eaten the dinner which Porthos had ordered for three other people who had, by rather good luck, been prevented from attending. Now all Porthos had to do was to instruct his servant Mousqueton to double the number of wine bottles, and this was duly done by Mousqueton using a lasso to draw them up through the trap-door to the cellar. In the following deal Porthos doubled d'Artagnan who, on his way to a slam, had stopped at 5 ♠.

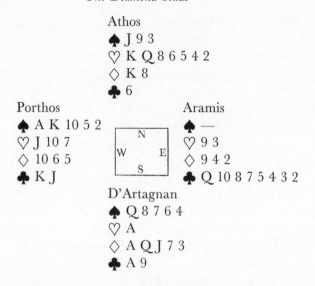

Athos
♠ J 9 3
♡ K Q 8 6 5 4 2
◇ K 8
♣ 6

Porthos
♠ A K 10 5 2
♡ J 10 7
◇ 10 6 5
♣ K J

Aramis
♠ —
♡ 9 3
◇ 9 4 2
♣ Q 10 8 7 5 4 3 2

D'Artagnan
♠ Q 8 7 6 4
♡ A
◇ A Q J 7 3
♣ A 9

Porthos led the ♡ J. As Porthos had by now become extremely cautious in his doubling of d'Artagnan it was clear that he must be very strong in trumps, and when d'Artagnan played the ♠ 4 and Porthos covered it with only the ♠ 5 d'Artagnan finessed with the ♠ 9. It was then that he found out *how* bad the trump situation was. D'Artagnan immediately now threw the ♣ 9 on the ♡ K, ruffed the ♡ Q with the ♠ 6, cashed three rounds of diamonds which Porthos had to follow, then the ◇ J, Porthos throwing the ♣ J and dummy a heart, and finally the last diamond which Porthos ruffed with the ♠ 2 and dummy overruffed with the ♠ 3. D'Artagnan returned to the closed hand with the ♣ A and played the ♠ 7. The ♠ J still remaining in dummy, Porthos won only two tricks of the ♠ A–K–10.

D'Artagnan told him that if he had on the second (or the first) trick taken the ♠ K and then continued with the ♠ A and the ♠ 2 he would have been sitting pretty with the guarded ♠ 10!

North/Both.

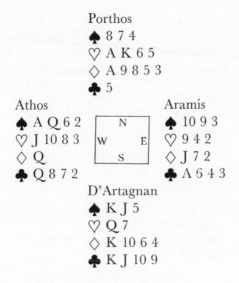

Porthos
♠ 8 7 4
♡ A K 6 5
◇ A 9 8 5 3
♣ 5

Athos
♠ A Q 6 2
♡ J 10 8 3
◇ Q
♣ Q 8 7 2

Aramis
♠ 10 9 3
♡ 9 4 2
◇ J 7 2
♣ A 6 4 3

D'Artagnan
♠ K J 5
♡ Q 7
◇ K 10 6 4
♣ K J 10 9

The bidding:	North	South
	1 ♡	2 NT
	3 ◇	3 NT

Athos led his lowest club. Aramis won with the ace and continued with the ♣ 3. Athos won with the ♣ Q and exited in clubs. From dummy d'Artagnan threw two spades. Clearly, he did not want to give Aramis the opportunity of playing spades. When, consequently, the ◇ Q fell on the ◇ 4 to the ace, d'Artagnan finessed a diamond through Aramis. When this succeeded he cashed the remaining diamonds. Then he entered the closed hand on the ♡ Q to cash the ♣ 9. Since he had to keep three hearts Athos jettisoned the ♠ A. That made no difference because d'Artagnan in any event would take the rest of the tricks.

On his return to Paris d'Artagnan was summoned to the presence of Cardinal Richelieu. His immediate thought was that he would be placed under arrest for having crossed that powerful minister. But later in the evening, in the rue Férou, he was able to tell his friends that all the Cardinal had done was to offer him entry in his service as an ensign in the guards. He had had no hesitation in declining for, as he said, all his friends were musketeers and all his enemies were in the guards. On that they all adjourned to the bridge table.

North/Love all.

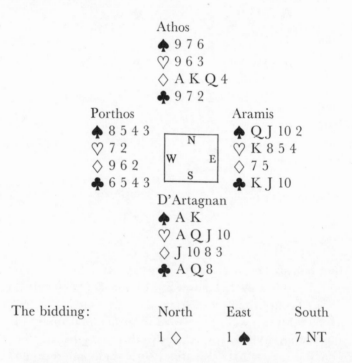

Athos
♠ 9 7 6
♡ 9 6 3
◇ A K Q 4
♣ 9 7 2

Porthos
♠ 8 5 4 3
♡ 7 2
◇ 9 6 2
♣ 6 5 4 3

Aramis
♠ Q J 10 2
♡ K 8 5 4
◇ 7 5
♣ K J 10

D'Artagnan
♠ A K
♡ A Q J 10
◇ J 10 8 3
♣ A Q 8

The bidding:	North	East	South
	1 ◇	1 ♠	7 NT

Athos' opening bid was a very weak one, and Aramis' defensive bid was not all that much better. But d'Artagnan had his own good reasons for putting more faith in Athos than in Aramis.

Porthos led the ♠ 8. For a player of d'Artagnan's ability it could, on occasion, be easy enough to count up to thirteen tricks in not much more than a minute. He won the first trick with the ♠ K. And twice he went to dummy by overtaking the ◇ 8 and ◇ 10 to finesse hearts. The diamond distribution proving to be 3–2 he could also overtake the ◇ J for the third heart finesse. Then he cashed the ♡ A and the ♠ A—the 'Vienne Coup'—before he played the ◇ 3 to dummy's ◇ 4. On the third diamond Aramis had to throw a spade, and he was now helpless. In order not to set up dummy's ♠ 9 he had to drop a club, whereupon d'Artagnan finished with three club tricks, the king, of course, being finessed.

For all that he had achieved for her the Queen rewarded d'Artagnan with a diamond ring and allowed him to kiss her hand. But the reward he wanted most of all was a meeting with Constance Bonacieux, for he had made no secret that he was in love with her. This could not, however, be arranged. A second trap had been set for her and she had disappeared. In a bad mood, therefore, he went to the rue Férou where he was warmly welcomed by his three friends who were wanting him for a rubber.

South/Love all.

Athos
♠ 8 7 5
♡ A 9 3
◇ A K 9 4 2
♣ J 7

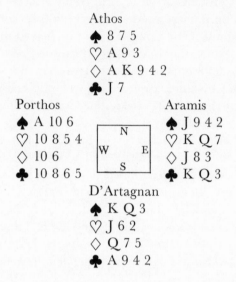

Porthos
♠ A 10 6
♡ 10 8 5 4
◇ 10 6
♣ 10 8 6 5

Aramis
♠ J 9 4 2
♡ K Q 7
◇ J 8 3
♣ K Q 3

D'Artagnan
♠ K Q 3
♡ J 6 2
◇ Q 7 5
♣ A 9 4 2

The bidding:	South	North
	1 ♣	1 ◇
	1 NT	3 NT

D'Artagnan's mood was caused not only by being unable to meet Constance—recently he had been dealt some very poor cards. His present hand was the nearest to an opening bid, even if a bad one.

Porthos led his lowest heart and Aramis, cunning as he could be, overplayed himself. Trying to fool d'Artagnan he won with the ♡ K, after dummy had followed with the ♡ 3. But it was only Porthos who was taken in, because when Aramis shifted to the ♠ 2 and Porthos took d'Artagnan's king with the ace he did not return to hearts but continued with the ♠ 10. D'Artagnan could only see eight tricks having found the ♠ A on the wrong side. But now he got his chance —he won with the ♠ Q and quickly cashed five rounds of diamonds. On the two last of these Aramis threw a spade and a club. D'Artagnan cashed the ♣ A and then played a spade. After having cashed the ♣ K Aramis played the ♡ 7 with the most innocent air in the world, but d'Artagnan had seen through him. He went up with the ♡ J and as it held, as he expected it would, the contract was made.

There was nothing unfair in what Aramis had done, but it gave d'Artagnan infinite pleasure to beat him at his own game.

South/Both.

Porthos
♠ 7 5 3
♡ 9 4
◇ J 10 5
♣ K J 7 5 4

D'Artagnan
♠ Q J 9
♡ 10 7 6 5
◇ 7 6 2
♣ Q 8 6

Athos
♠ 6 4 2
♡ 8 3 2
◇ 9 8 4 3
♣ 10 9 3

Aramis
♠ A K 10 8
♡ A K Q J
◇ A K Q
♣ A 2

The bidding:	South	North
	2 ♣	2 ◇
	2 ♡	3 ♣
	4 NT	5 ♣
	5 NT	6 ◇
	7 NT	

D'Artagnan led the ♠ J and Aramis, winning with the ace, had a strong suspicion that d'Artagnan was trying 'the old trick'—the jack from the Q–J doubleton. So, before putting his trust in the club suit he cashed the ♠ K. D'Artagnan, who had seen at a glance the danger of his ♣ Q and knowing what Aramis didn't know that the clubs would provide sufficient tricks, decided to confirm Aramis in his suspicion and dropped the ♠ Q! Triumphantly Aramis burst out:

'Didn't I know it was 'the old trick'!'

Now he saw no reason to risk the club finesse but entered dummy with the ♣ K to finesse for the ♠ 9. But d'Artagnan took the ♠ 8 with the ♠ 9, and the cold grand slam went down.

South/Both.

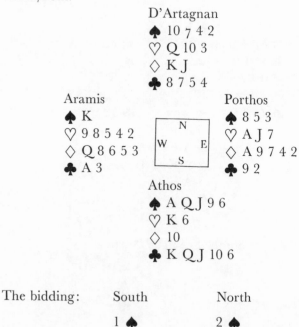

D'Artagnan
♠ 10 7 4 2
♡ Q 10 3
◇ K J
♣ 8 7 5 4

Aramis
♠ K
♡ 9 8 5 4 2
◇ Q 8 6 5 3
♣ A 3

Porthos
♠ 8 5 3
♡ A J 7
◇ A 9 7 4 2
♣ 9 2

Athos
♠ A Q J 9 6
♡ K 6
◇ 10
♣ K Q J 10 6

The bidding:	South	North
	1 ♠	2 ♠
	4 ♠	

Aramis opened with the ♣ A and continued with the ♣ 3, even though Porthos followed with the ♣ 2. Athos won and led the ◇ 10 to dummy's king. Porthos took the trick with the ace and returned another diamond which Athos ruffed. He tried the ♡ K, which Porthos let him win, and then the ♡ 6 to the queen. Porthos won and exited with the ♡ J which Athos ruffed. Porthos gave a malicious grin at having kept Athos out of dummy; but Athos then had to lay down the ♠ A dropping Aramis' king.

As Porthos had nothing which could be finessed there was absolutely no reason to try to block the dummy—quite the contrary. The least suspicious way to give dummy an entry would have been to show the doubleton club by dropping the ♣ 9 to the first trick, for Athos would then have unblocked the ♣ 10 and won the second trick with dummy's ♣ 8. He would then, doubtless, have taken the opportunity to finesse in trumps, and gone one down.

One of Aramis' less likeable methods was to sow dissension among his opponents—for when two partners are quarrelling neither of them benefits. The following deal shows one of the more innocent ways of doing this. The hand was dealt after d'Artagnan had left Crèvecoeur, and so that a game still might be played Aramis told his servant, Bazin, despite his indignation, to take a hand.

East/N–S.

Bazin
♠ 10 9 6 3
♡ 6
♢ K J 5 3
♣ J 9 8 6

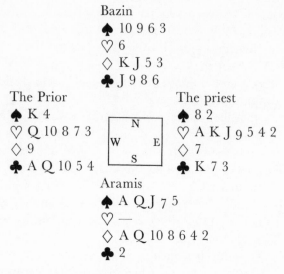

The Prior
♠ K 4
♡ Q 10 8 7 3
♢ 9
♣ A Q 10 5 4

The priest
♠ 8 2
♡ A K J 9 5 4 2
♢ 7
♣ K 7 3

Aramis
♠ A Q J 7 5
♡ —
♢ A Q 10 8 6 4 2
♣ 2

The bidding:

East	South	West	North
4 ♡	4 ♠	5 ♡	Pass
Pass	5 ♠		

The Prior led his singleton ♢ 9. Aramis won with dummy's
king and shifted to the ♠ 10 which went to the Prior's king.
The Prior shifted to the ♡ 7 which the priest took with the
♡ K, while Aramis dropped the ♣ 2! The idea was to give
the priest an opportunity *not* to play a diamond which the
Prior had omitted to do in the previous trick. Of course,
neither of them knew that the other was also void. And when
the expected diamond was not played by either the pair
became more and more irritable, and thus weakened their
play. Probably they did not find out until very much later
that North and South held eleven diamonds between them.
But the vital confidence between partners had been lost.

MILADY

Porthos was always boastful of the well-born people who were his intimate friends, and this particularly applied to a certain, but unnamed, Duchess. One day, purely out of curiosity, d'Artagnan followed him to church where he saw him make the pretence of bowing to a beautiful woman and also pretending to take no notice of an elderly woman who was showing signs of jealousy.

When the first left the church with her servant d'Artagnan followed them. He had the vague feeling that he recognised her, and that she was the person he saw when she parted from the comte de Rochefort at Meung. When the pair entered their carriage and moved off they met a horse-rider who was none other than Lord Winter, one of the Englishmen from Amiens. They had a brief whispered conversation. and she gently tapped him on the shoulder with her fan. D'Artagnan thought that it was a convenient moment to introduce himself. The ultimate outcome of this encounter with the lady and her friend was that there were duels between the four·friends and Lord Winter and three other Englishmen. The result was victory for the Frenchmen. In his own duel d'Artagnan merely disarmed his opponent, although in fact he could easily have killed him.

It was then that Lord Winter sought permission to introduce d'Artagnan to the lady who turned out to be his sister-in-law. And that was exactly what d'Artagnan wanted to find out. It was finally agreed that Lord Winter should later call for d'Artagnan at the address of Athos in the rue Férou. Pending that event the inevitable rubbers were played.

East/E–W

Athos
♠ 8 7 3
♡ A Q 10
♢ Q 5
♣ A K Q 10 5

Porthos
♠ 6 2
♡ 6 4 3
♢ J 7 3 2
♣ 9 7 4 3

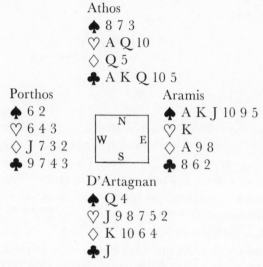

Aramis
♠ A K J 10 9 5
♡ K
♢ A 9 8
♣ 8 6 2

D'Artagnan
♠ Q 4
♡ J 9 8 7 5 2
♢ K 10 6 4
♣ J

The bidding:

East	South	West	North
1 ♠	Pass	Pass	2 ♣
2 ♠	3 ♡	Pass	4 ♡

Porthos led the ♠ 6. Aramis won with the ♠ K and continued with the ♠ A, Porthos following with the ♠ 2. D'Artagnan was ready with the ♡ 9 for the next spade, but when Aramis cashed the ♢ A and continued with another diamond to dummy's queen d'Artagnan claimed the rest saying:

'I am drawing three rounds of trumps from top.'

Aramis had to drop his blank king under the ace, and said querulously:

'How on earth could you know that the king was blank?'

'You were trying to be a little bit too clever,' was d'Artagnan's reply. 'When you didn't play a third round of spades it could only be because you would not disclose that Porthos couldn't overruff me, and that being the case you must have been holding the singleton ♡ K yourself. Had you held it guarded it would have cost you nothing to play a third spade after the ♠ A.'

South/E–W.

Athos
♠ K J 10
♡ K
♢ A 9 2
♣ A K Q J 9 4

Aramis
♠ Q 7 4 2
♡ 10 5 3
♢ K Q J 5
♣ 10 3

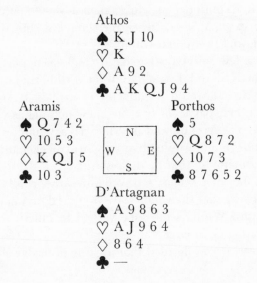

Porthos
♠ 5
♡ Q 8 7 2
♢ 10 7 3
♣ 8 7 6 5 2

D'Artagnan
♠ A 9 8 6 3
♡ A J 9 6 4
♢ 8 6 4
♣ —

The bidding:

South	North
1 ♠	3 ♣
3 ♡	3 ♠
4 ♡	6 ♠

Aramis led the ♢ K which was taken by dummy's ace. D'Artagnan was considering whether he should first draw two rounds of trumps, and then run the clubs, but a few seconds' thought were enough to decide on a better plan which could stand a 4–1 trump distribution. He cashed only two clubs to get rid of the losing diamonds, then led the ♠ J to the ace and the ♠ 3 back to the ♠ 10 which held. Porthos dropped a diamond. Then he ran the clubs. Aramis could certainly ruff with the ♠ 7, but whatever card he returned d'Artagnan would take the rest of the tricks.

'You were lucky to find the trump finesse,' remarked Aramis.

'Not at all,' d'Artagnan replied. 'If you are void on the second trump I can go up on the ♠ K and run the clubs. And if Porthos had been able to take the ♠ 10 with the queen, and continued in clubs, then I should have ruffed with the ♠ 8. As you can see the slam was cold when you both followed to the first trump.'

After a few uninteresting hands had been played Lord Winter arrived and d'Artagnan went with him to call on his sister-in-law. It would be difficult to explain d'Artagnan's interest in her, particularly as he knew nothing as yet about her shady background and past life. To say 'interest' would be not enough, nor would 'love' or a form of 'enchantment'—it was, put simply, that he desired her.

When they met Milady received him rather coldly. He was not yet aware that she would have preferred him not to have spared Lord Winter's life—she wished to inherit from him sooner rather than later.

However, it was decided that a game of bridge should be played.

East/Love all.

D'Artagnan
♠ J 10 9 8
♡ A K 5 4
◇ Q 6 4
♣ A K

Lord Summer
♠ Q 7
♡ J 9 6
◇ A K J 7 5 3
♣ J 10

Lord Winter
♠ K 6 5
♡ 10 8 3 2
◇ 9 8
♣ 9 8 4 2

Milady
♠ A 4 3 2
♡ Q 7
◇ 10 2
♣ Q 7 6 5 3

The bidding:

East	South	West	North
Pass	Pass	1 ◇	Dble.
Pass	1 ♠	2 ◇	3 ♠
Pass	4 ♠		

Lord Summer led the ◇ K. Most innocently, and with eyes that showed nothing of the destructive force within her, Milady 'unblocked' the ◇ Q from dummy. Lord Summer continued with the ◇ A and ◇ J. When Lord Winter threw a club she ruffed and entered dummy with the ♣ K to play the ♠ J and let it ride. Lord Summer won with the ♠ Q and continued in clubs, whereupon trumps were finessed again. Milady took the rest. It was not until then that Lord Winter, who had looked with contempt at Milady's discard of the ◇ Q, realised what would have happened if he had ruffed the ◇ J with the ♠ 5—then E–W would have won two trump tricks.

D'Artagnan had followed Milady's play with admiration, admitting to himself that he could not have done better. This increased his interest in her—an interest which would lead to a most desolate period in his life, she was to become his mortal enemy.

PREPARATIONS
FOR WAR

At this particular time Cardinal Richelieu was preparing for a campaign against the Huguenots in La Rochelle. In those days men in élite regiments had to provide their own equipment and maintain it. In d'Artagnan's case this was far less expensive than for the King's Musketeers. Money for all four's expenses had to be raised.

Milady, mistaking d'Artagnan for her lover de Wardes, had given him a ring which Athos recognised. When d'Artagnan described Milady to Athos the latter was perfectly sure that she was the woman he had married when he was a young man, and whom he had later discovered to be a branded criminal. With his status as a nobleman he was quite within his rights to have her hanged, but she had escaped this fate.

Naturally d'Artagnan wanted to return to Athos the ring which was, indeed, his own property. But Athos would have nothing of this, and the ring was sold to help with the provision of equipment. There was enough left over from the sale to buy a quantity of their favourite Anjou wine, and Athos invited his friends for drinks and bridge.

South/N–S.

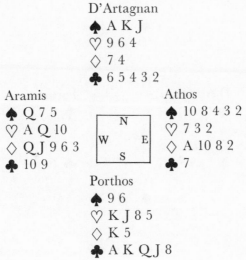

D'Artagnan
♠ A K J
♡ 9 6 4
◇ 7 4
♣ 6 5 4 3 2

Aramis
♠ Q 7 5
♡ A Q 10
◇ Q J 9 6 3
♣ 10 9

Athos
♠ 10 8 4 3 2
♡ 7 3 2
◇ A 10 8 2
♣ 7

Porthos
♠ 9 6
♡ K J 8 5
◇ K 5
♣ A K Q J 8

The bidding:

South	West	North	East
1 ♣	1 ◇	2 ♣	Pass
2 ♡	Pass	3 ♣	Pass
3 NT			

In an absent-minded way Aramis cashed the ♡ A, and then asked what was the contract. When he was told that it was 3 No Trumps he merely said:

'Is that so!' and promptly shifted to the ♠ 7. Porthos daren't finesse as a diamond from Athos could make things uncomfortable. So he went up with the ♠ K, cashed the five club tricks and entered dummy on the ♠ A so that he could play a heart. Aramis had given him the impression that a heart finesse was safe and that he needed only the two heart tricks. But Aramis took the ♡ J with the queen, cashed the ♠ Q and then shifted to a diamond. Athos took the ◇ A and two spades, and Porthos went two down!

North/Both.

Athos
♠ A 5 2
♡ A Q 8 4
◇ K J 8 7
♣ J 8

D'Artagnan
♠ 8 6 3
♡ 7 6 5
◇ 5 4 2
♣ Q 9 7 5

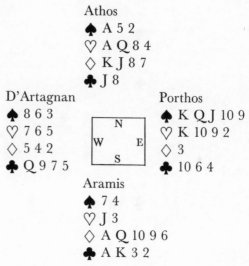

Porthos
♠ K Q J 10 9
♡ K 10 9 2
◇ 3
♣ 10 6 4

Aramis
♠ 7 4
♡ J 3
◇ A Q 10 9 6
♣ A K 3 2

The bidding:

North	East	South	West
1 ♡	1 ♠	2 ◇	Pass
2 NT	Pass	3 ♣	Pass
4 ◇	Pass	6 ◇	

D'Artagnan led the ♠ 8. Aramis, winning with dummy's ace, realised that the position was hopeless unless he could 'steal' a trick from Porthos who must surely be holding, he thought, the ♡ K for his intervening bid. At any rate there was nothing like trying and so he cashed the ♡ A and continued with the ♡ 4. Porthos, fearing that the ♡ Q would be established for a discard if his ♡ K was ruffed, ducked, and Aramis won the trick with the ♡ J. Now it was only necessary to ruff the two low clubs and then later lose a spade trick to Porthos.

Aramis thus to all intents and purposes 'stole' a trick, but it was for once quite honest.

West/E–W.

Aramis
♠ K 5
♡ K Q 9 6 2
♢ 10 7
♣ Q 8 5 3

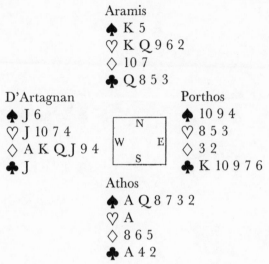

D'Artagnan
♠ J 6
♡ J 10 7 4
♢ A K Q J 9 4
♣ J

Porthos
♠ 10 9 4
♡ 8 5 3
♢ 3 2
♣ K 10 9 7 6

Athos
♠ A Q 8 7 3 2
♡ A
♢ 8 6 5
♣ A 4 2

The bidding:

West	North	East	South
1 ♢	1 ♡	Pass	2 ♠
Pass	3 ♠	Pass	4 ♠

D'Artagnan cashed the ♢ A–K and continued with the ♢ Q. Athos ruffed with dummy's ♠ K. Porthos, believing that Athos would ruff with the ♠ 5, 'overruffed' with the ♠ 9, but kept his blushes back when he found that the trick was not his. Athos drew the trumps and the ♡ A, after which he tried a club to the queen, but he had no luck—he had to lose two club tricks and went one down.

'Good for you, Porthos!' d'Artagnan cried.

'Don't laugh at me,' Porthos replied.

'I'm not laughing at you. If you had not got rid of that trump Athos would have cashed the ♡ A and endplayed you on the third trump. As it is you got two club tricks instead of the one trump trick.'

South/Both.

Athos
♠ A Q 10 8
♡ 10 6
◇ J 2
♣ J 10 7 5 3

Porthos
♠ K J 9 7
♡ 9 8 5
◇ K Q 9
♣ A K Q

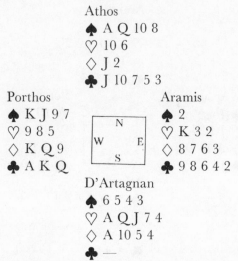

Aramis
♠ 2
♡ K 3 2
◇ 8 7 6 3
♣ 9 8 6 4 2

D'Artagnan
♠ 6 5 4 3
♡ A Q J 7 4
◇ A 10 5 4
♣ —

The bidding:

South	West	North	East
1 ♠ !	Dble.	3 ♠	Pass
4 ♠	Dble.	Pass	Pass
Redble.			

Porthos opened with the ♣ K which d'Artagnan ruffed.
Then he led the ♠ 4 and finessed with dummy's ♠ 8. As
Aramis followed with the ♠ 2 it was clear that Porthos held
the remaining trumps. From dummy the ♡ 10 was led,
followed by the ♡ 6 to the jack, and the ♡ A dropped the
king. The ♡ Q was ruffed by Porthos and overruffed in
dummy. A club was ruffed with the ♠ 5 to lead the fifth
heart, ruffed again by Porthos and overruffed in dummy.
D'Artagnan used his last trump to ruff a club, and the
situation became as follows:

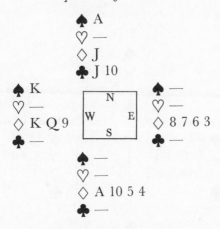

D'Artagnan played the ◇ 4 and Porthos saved a trick by going up with ◇ Q, but d'Artagnan took the rest and scored two redoubled overtricks.

A messenger arrived from the Duchesse de Chevreuse with money for Aramis for his equipment; it was much more than he needed. Porthos was relying on his elderly cousin, who was very much in love with him because she considered him to be such a dashing fellow. He simulated a return of affection purely and simply because of her husband's wealth and visited them as often as he could find sufficient excuse to do so. The couple lived in the rue des Ours, and Monsieur Coquenard only tolerated Porthos' visits because of the opportunity they gave him of playing bridge, for this was a ruling passion of his. On such occasions his chief clerk, Biquet, was called in as a fourth. The following hands were dealt at some of Porthos' visits:

South/E–W.

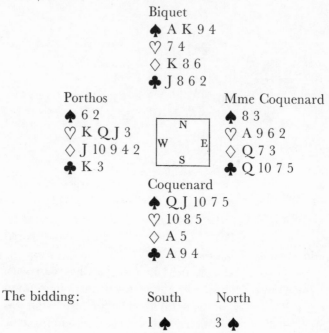

Biquet
♠ A K 9 4
♡ 7 4
◇ K 8 6
♣ J 8 6 2

Porthos
♠ 6 2
♡ K Q J 3
◇ J 10 9 4 2
♣ K 3

Mme Coquenard
♠ 8 3
♡ A 9 6 2
◇ Q 7 3
♣ Q 10 7 5

Coquenard
♠ Q J 10 7 5
♡ 10 8 5
◇ A 5
♣ A 9 4

The bidding:

	South	North
	1 ♠	3 ♠
	4 ♠	

Porthos led the ♡ K, then the ♡ Q, following which he shifted to the ◇ J which Coquenard took with the ace. He cashed the ♣ A, and since Porthos had placed the ♣ 3 between the ♠ 6 and the ♠ 2 his 'blank' king fell to the ace. Coquenard, hoping to find the ♣ K or the ♣ Q doubleton with East or West, had cashed the ♣ A so early in the play to deter his wife or Porthos from thinking of unblocking. He cashed two rounds of trumps, and it was then that Porthos discovered his 'error' and was most unhappy about it. Coquenard ruffed the ♡ 10, cashed the ◇ K, and ruffed dummy's last diamond. He followed on by leading the ♣ 4 in the hope that Parthos held the blank queen. If Porthos had now held the ♣ K he would have had to win and play a card for a ruff and discard, and thus Coquenard would have made his contract.

But thanks to the involuntary unblocking Madame Coquenard could now take two club tricks, and the contract went one down.

North/N–S.

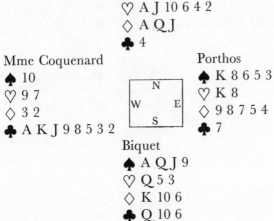

Coquenard
♠ 7 4 2
♡ A J 10 6 4 2
♢ A Q J
♣ 4

Mme Coquenard
♠ 10
♡ 9 7
♢ 3 2
♣ A K J 9 8 5 3 2

Porthos
♠ K 8 6 5 3
♡ K 8
♢ 9 8 7 5 4
♣ 7

Biquet
♠ A Q J 9
♡ Q 5 3
♢ K 10 6
♣ Q 10 6

Coquenard opened the bidding with 1 ♡, and Porthos felt bold enough to bid 1 ♠ which Biquet doubled. Coquenard, however, feeling no confidence in the double, bid 2 ♡, and Biquet promptly raised the bidding to 3 No Trumps.

Dutifully, Madame Coquenard led her singleton ♠ 10, her cousin's suit, but Biquet won the trick with the ♠ J. Seeing that he needed at least two heart tricks he played the ♡ Q and let it ride. Porthos took it with the ♡ K, and as the red suits looked just as hopeless as the spades he tried the ♣ 7— and to everyone's tremendous surprise Madame Coquenard then took the next eight tricks in clubs.

South/Love all.

Biquet
♠ J 10 9 6
♡ 7
◇ A Q J 6 3
♣ 6 5 3

Mme Coquenard
♠ A Q 7 4
♡ 10 5 2
◇ 8 7 5
♣ K 8 4

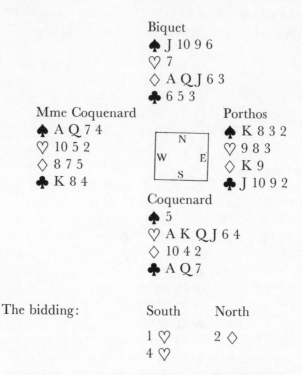

Porthos
♠ K 8 3 2
♡ 9 8 3
◇ K 9
♣ J 10 9 2

Coquenard
♠ 5
♡ A K Q J 6 4
◇ 10 4 2
♣ A Q 7

The bidding:

South	North
1 ♡	2 ◇
4 ♡	

Although the contract looks sound, the defence should be given a hard look. Madame Coquenard led the ♠ 4! Porthos winning with the ♠ K, shifted to the ♣ J. Coquenard took the losing finesse with the queen and had to win the next club with the ace. Having drawn trumps he had to try the diamond finesse, which lost, and Porthos took the undertrick with the ♣ 10.

'Why on earth did you lead that card?' grumbled Coquenard when he saw his wife's hand.

'I did what you have always taught me to do, and led my fourth-best spade,' was her reply.

North/N–S.

Porthos
♠ 10 6 2
♡ 10 4
♢ K 9 5 2
♣ 8 6 4 2

Biquet
♠ 7 3
♡ J 9 5 3 2
♢ 8 7 4
♣ J 10 9

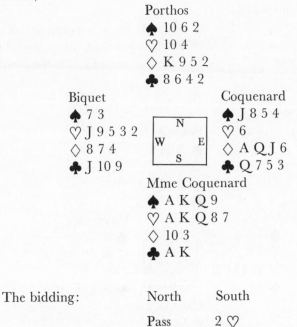

Coquenard
♠ J 8 5 4
♡ 6
♢ A Q J 6
♣ Q 7 5 3

Mme Coquenard
♠ A K Q 9
♡ A K Q 8 7
♢ 10 3
♣ A K

The bidding:	North	South
	Pass	2 ♡
	2 NT	3 ♠
	3 NT	4 ♡

Biquet opened with the ♣ J. Madame Coquenard won and immediately played the ♡ 7 to dummy's ♡ 10, Biquet ducking, to play the ♠ 2 from dummy and finesse with the ♠ 9. Then she drew three rounds of trumps and lost only one trump trick and two diamond tricks.

'Why did you have the brilliant idea to play a low heart, my dear cousin?' asked Porthos.

'Well, I had to enter dummy in order to finesse spades.'

'Finesse spades?'

'Yes, because you have yourself instructed me in the law of symmetry.'

'What on earth are you talking about?'

'Just this—when West holds the ♣ J then East must hold the ♠ J.'

'Then why didn't you try to enter dummy with the ◇ K?' her husband asked.

'No, not at all. I knew you held the ace because I saw distinctly that you didn't like the club lead. As you could want neither spades nor hearts, then it had to be diamonds you wanted!'

North/E–W.

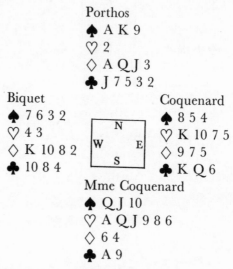

Porthos
♠ A K 9
♡ 2
◇ A Q J 3
♣ J 7 5 3 2

Biquet
♠ 7 6 3 2
♡ 4 3
◇ K 10 8 2
♣ 10 8 4

Coquenard
♠ 8 5 4
♡ K 10 7 5
◇ 9 7 5
♣ K Q 6

Mme Coquenard
♠ Q J 10
♡ A Q J 9 8 6
◇ 6 4
♣ A 9

The bidding:

North	East	South	West
1 ♣	Pass	2 ♡	Pass
3 NT	Pass	6 ♡	Pass
Pass	Dble.		

Biquet led the ♠ 7 and after much thought Madame Coquenard considered that she had only a chance if Biquet held the ◇ K. So she won with the ♠ Q and tried the diamond finesse, which held. She then played dummy's ♡ 2 and thought hard about the deep finesse—but found it too dangerous as Biquet might be holding the singleton ♡ 10.

She won with the ♡ J and cashed the ♡ A to see what happened. Nothing happened except that Biquet followed again. It was evident that Coquenard could only have started with the ♡ K–10–7–5; he could not in any case have held less, and his double was bad enough even with that.

Madame Coquenard now quickly cashed the ♣ A, played the ♢ 6 to the queen, threw the ♣ 9 on the ♢ A, ruffed a club, led a spade to the king to ruff another club, and finally played a spade to the ace. Coquenard's two last cards were the ♡ K–10, and his wife held the ♡ Q–9. The lead being from dummy Coquenard could only take one trick.

'You were too greedy, my good man,' his wife said. 'If you hadn't doubled I would have played three rounds of trumps and gone down.'

When Porthos was finally successful in getting his cousin to open her purse, with the result that the financial position of the four friends had been considerably brightened, Porthos made the acceptable suggestion that they should have luncheon at 'La Corne d'Abondance'. The name alone appealed to the food-loving musketeer, and the meal fulfilling all their expectations they subsequently visited it quite often. Readers of Dumas' 'La Dame de Monsoreau' may well remember the name, for it was in this restaurant that Chicot and Dom Gorenflot often ate their gargantuan meals.

During their later visits the following hands were dealt:

South/N–S.

Aramis
♠ A 7 3
♡ A Q 4
◇ 8 7 6 4
♣ K 8 6

Athos   D'Artagnan
♠ Q 9 8 6   ♠ 10 5 2
♡ J 10 7 3   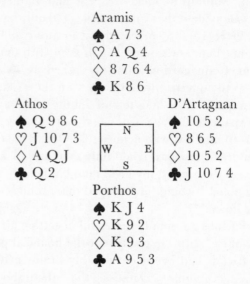   ♡ 8 6 5
◇ A Q J   ◇ 10 5 2
♣ Q 2   ♣ J 10 7 4

Porthos
♠ K J 4
♡ K 9 2
◇ K 9 3
♣ A 9 5 3

The bidding:

South	West	North	East
1 ♣	Dble.	Redble.	Pass
Pass	1 ♠	Pass	Pass
1 NT	Pass	3 NT	

Athos opened with the ♡ 3. Porthos won with dummy's
ace to play the ♣ 6 and let it ride to Athos' ♣ Q. Athos then
led another heart. This time Porthos took the king in the
closed hand and cashed the ♣ K and the ♣ A, but as Athos
threw the ♠ 6 on the third club Porthos entered dummy on
the ♡ A and, without any great hope, led a diamond to the
◇ 9. Athos won with the ◇ J, cashed the ♡ J and shifted to
the ♠ 8. This was what Porthos had been waiting for—he
could assuredly cash three spade tricks, but after that he had
to lose two diamonds to Athos, and went one down.

Porthos then asked whether he could have made the
contract.

'Yes,' d'Artagnan at once replied. 'After the double and the opening lead it was clear that Athos held four spades and four hearts and, therefore, four diamonds and one club, or, three diamonds and two clubs, together with all the high cards. The chance of establishing the fourth diamond was therefore better than the fourth club. So you should have at once attacked the diamonds and later on endplay Athos so that he had then had to lead spades into your tenace. And thus to the second trick you should lead a diamond. Athos wins and continues in hearts, and then it should be time for you to cash the third heart and the ♣ A–K before continuing in diamonds. As a matter of fact you did have the right idea —but you should not have given us that club trick.'

East/Love all.

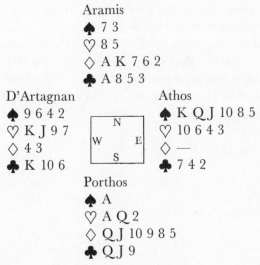

Aramis
♠ 7 3
♡ 8 5
◇ A K 7 6 2
♣ A 8 5 3

D'Artagnan
♠ 9 6 4 2
♡ K J 9 7
◇ 4 3
♣ K 10 6

Athos
♠ K Q J 10 8 5
♡ 10 6 4 3
◇ —
♣ 7 4 2

Porthos
♠ A
♡ A Q 2
◇ Q J 10 9 8 5
♣ Q J 9

The bidding:

East	South	West	North
3 ♠	4 ◇	4 ♠	4 NT
Pass	5 ♡	Pass	6 ◇

East–West have a good sacrifice in 6 ♠ which would only go three down, but d'Artagnan calculated on a sure trick on at least one of the kings as well as on Porthos making an error so that he got a second trick. Instead he led the ♠ 9. Porthos won and drew two rounds of trumps after which he tried the heart finesse, which he lost. He ruffed the next spade, cashed the ♡ A and then ruffed a heart. Following that he finessed clubs both ways so that d'Artagnan got the setting trick with the ♣ 10.

'There was nothing else I could do,' Porthos lamented. 'Both the ♡ K and the ♣ 10 were wrong.'

'On the contrary, my good friend,' replied d'Artagnan. 'In point of fact we had given you too much information. After the bidding Athos had a lot of spades and nothing else, so that when I raise I must hold one of the kings or, still better, both of them. After having drawn the trumps you should have ruffed dummy's last spade and played the clubs so that I would win the third round and would not be able to exit in clubs. Thus the ♣ 10 was the key card, but if Athos should have been holding it you would still have the heart finesse as a last chance. Only if that too should lose you could be certain that there was nothing to be done.'

South/Love all.

Aramis
♠ 9
♡ K 5 4 2
♢ A Q 8
♣ K Q 10 8 2

D'Artagnan
♠ Q J 10 4
♡ A Q 3
♢ J 10 4 2
♣ 7 5

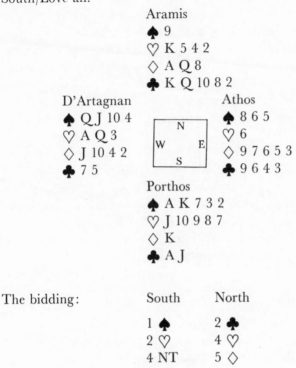

Athos
♠ 8 6 5
♡ 6
♢ 9 7 6 5 3
♣ 9 6 4 3

Porthos
♠ A K 7 3 2
♡ J 10 9 8 7
♢ K
♣ A J

The bidding:

	South	North
	1 ♠	2 ♣
	2 ♡	4 ♡
	4 NT	5 ♢
	6 ♡	

D'Artagnan led the ♡ A and, after having seen dummy, continued with the ♡ 3. As one never leads from A–Q behind the declarer Athos, naturally, must hold the ♡ Q so that it was in order for Porthos to go up with dummy's king, but no queen dropped! Another clever piece of play by d'Artagnan, and one that was not easy to see through. Of course, if the ♡ K had not been in dummy he would not have continued trumps. And if d'Artagnan had not led trumps at all, then Porthos would doubtless have played on finessing the queen.

North/Both.

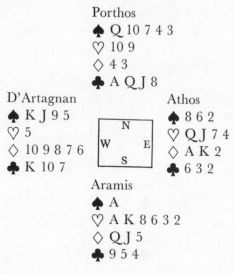

Porthos
♠ Q 10 7 4 3
♡ 10 9
◇ 4 3
♣ A Q J 8

D'Artagnan
♠ K J 9 5
♡ 5
◇ 10 9 8 7 6
♣ K 10 7

Athos
♠ 8 6 2
♡ Q J 7 4
◇ A K 2
♣ 6 3 2

Aramis
♠ A
♡ A K 8 6 3 2
◇ Q J 5
♣ 9 5 4

The bidding:

North	South
Pass	1 ♡
1 ♠	2 ♡
3 ♣	4 ♡

D'Artagnan led the ◇ 10 and Athos cashed his two diamond tricks. It was clear that Aramis held the ◇ Q and Athos could also see the clubs in order. The question now was how to get two trump tricks.

Athos solved the problem by leading the ♣ 2 right into the tenace in dummy. D'Artagnan played the ♣ 10, taken by dummy's ♣ J, and the ♡ 10 was led from dummy. Athos followed with the ♡ 7. Aramis went up with the ace and also cashed the ♡ K. He dared not take the double finesse and run the risk that d'Artagnan would win the first trick, for Athos' ♣ 2 smelled dangerously of a singleton. It was thus that Athos got his two trump tricks to set the contract.

West/Both.

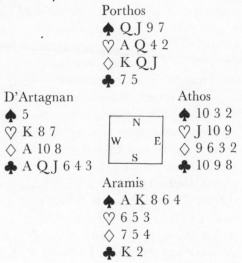

Porthos
♠ Q J 9 7
♡ A Q 4 2
◇ K Q J
♣ 7 5

D'Artagnan
♠ 5
♡ K 8 7
◇ A 10 8
♣ A Q J 6 4 3

Athos
♠ 10 3 2
♡ J 10 9
◇ 9 6 3 2
♣ 10 9 8

Aramis
♠ A K 8 6 4
♡ 6 5 3
◇ 7 5 4
♣ K 2

The bidding:

West	North	East	South
1 ♣	Dble.	Pass	2 ♠
Dble.	Redble.	3 ♣	Pass
Pass	4 ♠		

D'Artagnan led the ◇ A and continued with the ◇ 10 to
dummy's queen. Aramis gave careful thought to the situation. He was only too well aware that d'Artagnan held all the
high cards and that if Athos could get the lead and shift to
clubs there would be four losers. The essential thing to do was
to lead hearts twice from the closed hand and to take care that
d'Artagnan won the third heart, or to let him win the king if
he played it earlier. But as d'Artagnan very probably held a
singleton trump he would be able to unblock the ♡ K when
Aramis played the second trump to the closed hand.

A better idea would be to cash the ♡ A first, lead a trump
to the king and then a low heart up to the queen. If it had
been Porthos sitting West Aramis would certainly have used

this plan, but d'Artagnan's needle-sharp brain would almost certainly see through it all and let him unblock the ♡ K under the ace. Just then Aramis glanced out of the window to see a lovely woman entering her carriage. He innocently said:

'Isn't that one of your duchesses, Porthos?'

When Porthos turned round to look, and in doing so could not stop him, Aramis led the ♡ 6 from the closed hand. It was done so guilelessly that, just for once, d'Artganan was caught by the trap; when Aramis, with seeming reluctance, had to play hearts from dummy and cashed the ace, d'Artagnan still had no suspicion and saw no reason to unblock. Then a trump was played to the king and a heart from the closed hand, and without allowing Athos to get on lead the fourth heart was established for a club discard.

Readers of 'La Dame de Monsoreau' might care to be reminded here that it was also at the 'La Corne d'Abondance' that Chicot settled his difference with Borromé, one of de Guise's leaguers. Borromé thought that he had caught Chicot in ambush—on the contrary, Chicot was the victor. Borromé was a fencing-master who had instructed a young priest named Jacques Clément how to handle a dagger and it was he who assassinated Henri III.

LA ROCHELLE

When the siege of La Rochelle opened d'Artagnan had still not yet become a musketeer, and it was because of this that he had had to set out from Paris before his friends. Nevertheless, as will be remembered, the three musketeers arrived in camp just in time to prevent d'Artagnan drinking the poisoned wine which had been sent to him by Milady in the name of his friends. They were all soon able to relax, however, and once again the cards were being dealt.

South/Love all.

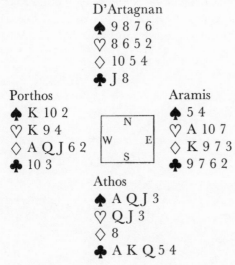

D'Artagnan
♠ 9 8 7 6
♡ 8 6 5 2
◇ 10 5 4
♣ J 8

Porthos
♠ K 10 2
♡ K 9 4
◇ A Q J 6 2
♣ 10 3

Aramis
♠ 5 4
♡ A 10 7
◇ K 9 7 3
♣ 9 7 6 2

Athos
♠ A Q J 3
♡ Q J 3
◇ 8
♣ A K Q 5 4

The bidding:

South	West	North	East
1 ♣	1 ♦	Pass	Pass
1 ♠	Pass	Pass	2 ♦
Pass	Pass	2 ♠	Pass
Pass	3 ♦	Pass	Pass
3 ♠	Dble.		

Porthos cashed the ♦ A and continued with the ♦ 2 to Aramis' king, Athos ruffing. He foresaw that he would get into difficulties if he drew the ♠ A and the ♠ Q. A finesse was considered to be a losing proposition if, as no doubt he did, Porthos held the king, and the only hope was that he held only three trumps—even then he would, when winning with the ♠ K, lead a third diamond, which would cost Athos' last trump and establish Porthos' ♠ 10. So there was nothing else to do but to try to lead Porthos on and win a tempo—Athos played the ♠ J!

Porthos thought that the trick for the ♠ K could never run away from him, and he ducked in case Aramis should be holding the singleton ♠ A or the ♠ Q. But the contract was saved. Athos cashed the ♠ A and played clubs until Porthos found it convenient to ruff with the ♠ K. Athos still held a trump to stop the diamonds, and East–West could take only two heart tricks.

West/N–S.

D'Artagnan
♠ J 4
♡ 10 4 3
◇ A 6 2
♣ A 9 8 5 3

Porthos
♠ 5
♡ A K Q J 6
◇ Q 9 7 5 4
♣ K 6

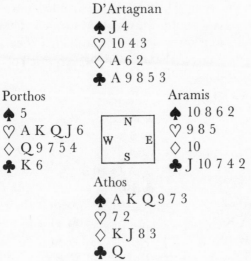

Aramis
♠ 10 8 6 2
♡ 9 8 5
◇ 10
♣ J 10 7 4 2

Athos
♠ A K Q 9 7 3
♡ 7 2
◇ K J 8 3
♣ Q

The bidding:

West	North	East	South
1 ♡	Pass	Pass	2 ♠
3 ◇	3 ♠	Pass	4 ♠

Porthos cashed the ♡ K and A and continued with the ♡ Q. Do you imagine that Athos ruffed? He certainly did not; he threw the ◇ 8. Porthos wondered what on earth was the idea and came to the conclusion that Athos did not hold enough trumps to afford to ruff, and that diamonds were his weakness. He therefore hastened to shift to the ◇ 5. Athos won the trick with the ◇ J, and now he could draw trumps and claim. As a result of Porthos' diamond bid Athos could see that he would scarcely be able to avoid two diamond losers with normal play, and so he might just as well lose one diamond at once and await the effect on Porthos.

There was one occasion when, everything being quiet in the camp, the four friends had gone out to the fields. They were preoccupied in reading a letter that had come from

Marie Michon and did not notice Cardinal Richelieu's arrival on the scene. The Cardinal demanded to see the letter and there was an argument, which Athos won. They had left their cards lying on a drum and although they felt a bit dispirited they agreed that they might just as well play a hand.

North/Love all.

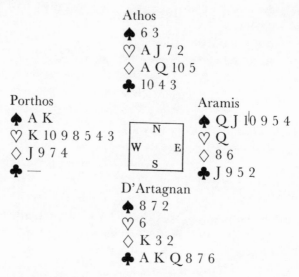

Athos
♠ 6 3
♡ A J 7 2
◇ A Q 10 5
♣ 10 4 3

Porthos
♠ A K
♡ K 10 9 8 5 4 3
◇ J 9 7 4
♣ —

Aramis
♠ Q J 10 9 5 4
♡ Q
◇ 8 6
♣ J 9 5 2

D'Artagnan
♠ 8 7 2
♡ 6
◇ K 3 2
♣ A K Q 8 7 6

The bidding:

North	East	South	West
1 ◇	1 ♠	2 ♣	2 ♡
Pass	Pass	5 ♣	Dble.

Porthos cashed two spades and then shifted to the ♡ 10. D'Artagnan won with dummy's ace and led the ♣ 3 to the ace. Probably one of todays' champion players would have gone into a long train of thought, and in the end would have forgotten exactly what he was thinking about—and misplayed the hand. Not so d'Artagnan, however, who took just ten seconds to reason out the following:

1   that he could not ruff his third spade without losing a trump trick;

2   that it was necessary to lead trumps twice from dummy to finesse the J–9;

3   that this needed two entries to dummy;

4   that a third entry was necessary to throw a spade on the fourth diamond; and

5   that Porthos had to hold the ◇ J if his plan should succeed.

As a consequence d'Artagnan played the ◇ 2 for the so-called 'unnecessary' finesse with the ◇ 10! Aramis covered the ♣ 10 with the ♣ J. D'Artagnan won with the queen, played the ◇ 3 to the queen to finesse clubs once again and drew all the trumps. Porthos' three last cards were the ♡ K and the ◇ J–9, and in dummy were the ♡ J and the ◇ A–5. In the closed hand d'Artagnan held the ♠ 8, the ◇ K and the ♣ 6. When d'Artagnan played his last trump Porthos was helpless and no matter what he did he couldn't win a trick.

After d'Artagnan's and the three musketeers' exploits at the Bastion Saint-Gervais the former was appointed to the Musketeers and all four of them spent whatever free hours they had playing cards in the inn 'Le Parpaillot'.

South/Both.

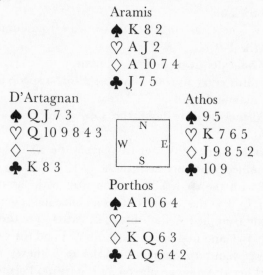

Aramis
♠ K 8 2
♡ A J 2
◇ A 10 7 4
♣ J 7 5

D'Artagnan
♠ Q J 7 3
♡ Q 10 9 8 4 3
◇ —
♣ K 8 3

Athos
♠ 9 5
♡ K 7 6 5
◇ J 9 8 5 2
♣ 10 9

Porthos
♠ A 10 6 4
♡ —
◇ K Q 6 3
♣ A Q 6 4 2

The bidding:

South	West	North	East
1 ♣	1 ♡	2 NT	Pass
3 ♠	Pass	4 ♠	

If one looks at the North–South hands it seems as if 6 ◇ might be a reasonable contract, but with the bad diamond break it was lucky for Porthos and Aramis that they did not bid higher.

D'Artagnan opened with the ♡ 10. Porthos realised how important it was to have the clubs established so long as the hearts were stopped, and at the same time it was essential to guard himself against an eventual 4–2 trump distribution. So he ruffed with the ♠ 4 in the closed hand, led the ♠ 6 to the king and the ♣ 5 to the ♣ Q. D'Artagnan won (there was no advantage to him in waiting) and continued in hearts. Porthos again ruffed in the closed hand and cashed the ♠ A, with the situation now being:

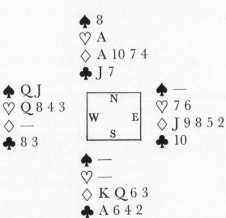

Porthos played three rounds of clubs, and d'Artagnan was helpless. He could ruff and draw dummy's last trump, but the ♡ A was still stopping the suit, and if he did not draw the last trump he would have to use it on a club or diamond, whereupon dummy's ♠ 8 would take over stopping the hearts.

East/Both.

The bidding:

East	South	West	North
1 ♠	Dble.	Pass	2 ◇
Pass	2 ♡	Pass	3 ♡
Pass	4 ♡		

Porthos led the ♠ 10 and Aramis won the trick with the ♠ J. He at once attacked trumps by leading a low trump to the king. While most players in East's position would take the trick with the ace and thus compel the declarer to draw his partner's jack, d'Artagnan had thought things out very quickly and, without any hesitation, ducked with the ♡ 4! Aramis continued with a heart from dummy, and as d'Artagnan ducked again it was perfectly logical to finesse with the ♡ 10 because Porthos must be holding either the blank ace or both the ♡ A and J, and in the latter case it didn't much matter what he did. However, it *did* matter— Porthos took the trick with the ♡ J, and d'Artagnan was able to score his three aces.

South/Both.

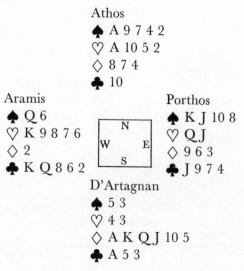

Athos
♠ A 9 7 4 2
♡ A 10 5 2
◇ 8 7 4
♣ 10

Aramis
♠ Q 6
♡ K 9 8 7 6
◇ 2
♣ K Q 8 6 2

Porthos
♠ K J 10 8
♡ Q J
◇ 9 6 3
♣ J 9 7 4

D'Artagnan
♠ 5 3
♡ 4 3
◇ A K Q J 10 5
♣ A 5 3

The bidding: South   North
                      1 ♢   1 ♠
                      3 ♢   3 ♡
                      4 NT   5 ♡
                      6 ♢

   As usual d'Artagnan was an optimist, in fact too optimistic,
but he loved to live dangerously. Aramis led the ♣ K, and
d'Artagnan won with the ace. He quickly saw that the spade
suit in dummy was his opportunity. So he led the ♠ 5, and
ducked with the ♠ 2 from dummy. Porthos won and hastened
to shift to a trump, but d'Artagnan now had the time to ruff
the ♣ 3 with the ♢ 7, cash the ♠ A, ruff the ♠ 4 with the
♢ 10, ruff the ♣ 5 with the ♢ 8 and the ♠ 7 with the ♢ J.
After that the remainder of the trumps, and dummy took the
last two tricks on the ♡ A and the ♠ 9.
   'But you cannot make with a trump lead,' Porthos said.
   'Of course not,' d'Artagnan replied, 'but when a trump had
not been led originally it is too late to shift. You, my dear
fellow, you should instead have shifted to the ♡ Q. Then I
could certainly have established the fifth spade, but I was
missing the ♡ A as an entry to cash it.'

North/Love all.

Aramis
♠ A J
♡ A K Q 10
♢ A Q 9 7 5
♣ A K

D'Artagnan
♠ Q 8 5 3
♡ 6 2
♢ J 10 6 2
♣ 10 4 2

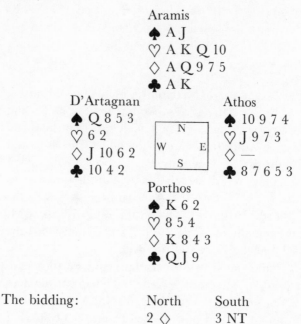

Athos
♠ 10 9 7 4
♡ J 9 7 3
♢ —
♣ 8 7 6 5 3

Porthos
♠ K 6 2
♡ 8 5 4
♢ K 8 4 3
♣ Q J 9

The bidding:

North	South
2 ♢	3 NT
7 NT	

D'Artagnan led the ♠ 3, and as one of Porthos' habits is to finesse queens, especially when the finesse is gratis, as it apparently was in this case, he tried dummy's ♠ J. Athos followed with the ♠ 4 and Porthos with the ♠ 2, remarking:

'I've fourteen tricks now.'

It didn't take long for d'Artagnan to reply:

'And that we will have to find out, my friend. I have the feeling that your fourteenth trick will cost you the twelfth and the thirteenth.'

Porthos cashed the ♠ A, the ♣ A–K and the ♡ A–K–Q and then played the ♢ 5 to the king to discover the unlucky diamond situation. On the ♠ K and the ♣ Q he threw dummy's ♡ 10 and ♢ 7. He then played the ♢ 3. D'Artagnan covered with the ♢ 10, and it was now that Porthos was missing the spade entry to the closed hand for the second finesse in diamonds. He would have had this second entry if he had gone up with the ♠ A on the first trick. He would certainly have lost the fourteenth trick for the ♠ J, but two extra diamond tricks would have given him the contract.

South/N–S.

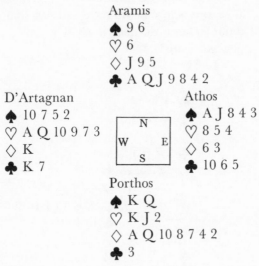

Aramis
♠ 9 6
♡ 6
◇ J 9 5
♣ A Q J 9 8 4 2

D'Artagnan
♠ 10 7 5 2
♡ A Q 10 9 7 3
◇ K
♣ K 7

Athos
♠ A J 8 4 3
♡ 8 5 4
◇ 6 3
♣ 10 6 5

Porthos
♠ K Q
♡ K J 2
◇ A Q 10 8 7 4 2
♣ 3

The bidding:

South	West	North	East
1 ◇	1 ♡	2 ♣	Pass
2 NT	Pass	3 ◇	Pass
3 NT			

D'Artagnan led the ♡ 10 and Porthos won with the jack. Anyone with a little knowledge of safety play would now have played the ♣ 3 to dummy's ace and then pinned his faith on the diamond finesse—and would have gone four down. But Porthos was not the person to be satisfied with one club trick if two were at all possible. He certainly led the ♣ 3, but he finessed with the ♣ Q and cashed the ♣ A, and when the king dropped the two became seven. Having cashed the club tricks, and discarded all his spades and hearts. Porthos led the ◇ J from dummy. Athos followed with the ◇ 6, and Porthos was going to finesse again, but then he thought it wise to count his tricks. Seeing that he already had eight he reluctantly went up with the ◇ A—and took all thirteen tricks.

On one particular day Aramis had to leave on some business or other, but before he went he had just time to tell his friends about a fantastic deal he had recently played with three duchess friends:

West/E–W.

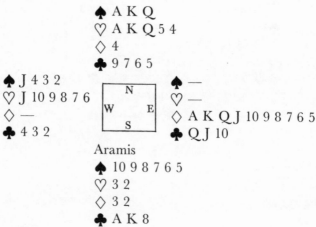

♠ A K Q
♡ A K Q 5 4
◇ 4
♣ 9 7 6 5

♠ J 4 3 2
♡ J 10 9 8 7 6
◇ —
♣ 4 3 2

♠ —
♡ —
◇ A K Q J 10 9 8 7 6 5
♣ Q J 10

Aramis
♠ 10 9 8 7 6 5
♡ 3 2
◇ 3 2
♣ A K 8

The bidding:

West	North	East	South
Pass	2 ♡	5 ◇	5 ♡
Dble.	Pass	Pass	5 ♠
Dble.			

West led the ♡ J, and Aramis won with dummy's ♡ Q, East dropping the ◇ 5. Aramis told how he had tried to establish dummy's fourth club without letting East get on lead (by leading the suit twice from dummy) and how he, when this was impossible, had shortened his trump length.

To the admiration of the ladies he ended with what we today call a 'Coup du Diable'. He was very full of himself but came down to earth again quickly when Porthos interjected:

'Why do you always complicate matters? It would have been quite simple to cash the ♣ A–K and the ♡ A–K–Q, throw the ♣ 8 and ruff the ♣ 7. Then three rounds of trumps and discard a diamond on the good ♣ 9. Your opponents would get only the highest trump and a diamond trick!'

Aramis reddened and turned to Athos and d'Artagnan, but they only laughed, and d'Artagnan said:

'There was an even simpler way. It should not be everyone who would discover Porthos' method of establishing the ♣ 9 (and here Porthos pushed his chest out), nor is it absolutely necessary. Simply throw the club loser on the third heart, lose a diamond to East, and ruff the other diamond with one of the spade honours. That's the way my grandmother would have played.'

The Bastion Saint-Gervais exploit referred to earlier was the result of a bet with M. de Busigny and three other men. What was at stake was a dinner for eight at 'Le Parpaillot', and from that time de Busigny was a frequent and interested kibitzer when cards were being played. Thus, when Aramis had to leave, it was suggested that de Busigny should be his substitute, and to this de Busigny readily agreed.

North / E–W.

                              De Busigny
                              ♠ —
                              ♡ Q 4 3 2
                              ◇ A 10 8 2
                              ♣ A K 8 6 3

        Athos   D'Artagnan
        ♠ A 10 8 6 5 2   ♠ 7 3
        ♡ 8   ┌─────────┐   ♡ K J 10 7
        ◇ Q J 9 7 5   │   N   │   ◇ 6 4
        ♣ 7   │ W   E │   ♣ Q J 10 9 5
                              │   S   │
                              └─────────┘
                              Porthos
                              ♠ K Q J 9 4
                              ♡ A 9 6 5
                              ◇ K 3
                              ♣ 4 2

The bidding: North   South

                          1 ♣   1 ♠
                          2 ♣   2 ♡
                          4 ♡

Athos led his singleton ♣ 7 and Porthos went one down, taking one trick with a spade ruff, one spade trick, two diamond tricks, two club tricks, two club ruffs, the ♡ A— total, nine tricks.

'I think you should have made the contract,' de Busigny mildly said.

'Mordieu!' exclaimed Porthos, 'You show me how.'

'What's the lead?'

'Does it matter much? Let's say the ♣ 7.'

'I will win with the ace,' and de Busigny went on to explain: 'Then I will lead the ♡ 2 to the ace to draw West's lonely trump. Then the ♠ K, covered with the ace and ruffed with the ♡ 3. I cash the ♣ K, ruff a club with the ♡ 5, enter dummy with the ◇ A to ruff another club with the

♡ 6 and cash the ◇ K and ♠ Q. Then the ♠ J which East can ruff, *but* East must give dummy the thirteenth trick for the ♡ Q.'

Porthos was impressed as he listened, but Athos who had noticed that d'Artagnan was smiling to himself said:

'M. de Busigny, what to you think about having another bet? For my part I will bet a dozen bottles of the best Anjou wine on my friend d'Artagnan being able to make an over-trick.'

'Done!' de Busigny exclaimed, 'and I will lead the ♣ 7.'

'Right,' d'Artagnan said. 'First trick the ♣ A. Second the ♡ A. Third the ♣ K. The fourth club ruff. The fifth the ♠ K and the ruffing of the ♠ A. The sixth club ruff. The seventh the ◇ A. The eighth club ruff. The ninth the ◇ K. The tenth the ♠ Q. And after that the ♠ J—and the ♡ Q must win a trick. Very nearly your plan, but with one trick more.'

Both Porthos and de Busigny were very impressed. But Athos had been intently watching d'Artagnan, and saw him still smiling. Even without d'Artagnan's wonderfully quick power of analysis Athos could see that it was impossible to squeeze another trick out of the cards, and so he said:

'I'll give you another chance, M. de Busigny. I'm prepared to bet that d'Artagnan will set your 5 ♡.'

'Done again!' was de Busigny's reply.

'Very well then,' d'Artagnan replied. 'I lead the ♠ A! And you can see how generous I am. I've established three spade tricks for you.'

It is unnecessary to go into full details. Everyone could see that dummy was deprived too early of an entry, and thus it was impossible to ruff all the three small clubs. De Busigny was rather cross at having overlooked this variation, and Athos offered him another chance of revenge, betting that d'Artagnan could, all the same, make five tricks. De Busigny accepted with alacrity and led the ♠ A. D'Artagnan ruffed with the ♡ 2, played the ♡ 3 from dummy and took East's ♡ 10 with the ace, cashed the ♠ K, threw a club from dummy and played the ◇ K, the ◇ A and the ◇ 8 from dummy. The situation now was:

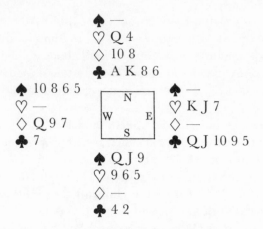

♠ —
♡ Q 4
◇ 10 8
♣ A K 8 6

♠ 10 8 6 5
♡ —
◇ Q 9 7
♣ 7

♠ —
♡ K J 7
◇ —
♣ Q J 10 9 5

♠ Q J 9
♡ 9 6 5
◇ —
♣ 4 2

'What are you going to do?' d'Artagnan asked M. de Busigny.

De Busigny thought aloud: 'If I throw a club you ruff, enter dummy on the ♣ A and then lead the ◇ 10. And if I duck you will ruff again, enter dummy on the ♣ K and ruff a club. So then I am down to three trumps. I must ruff your ♠ J and inevitably lose a trick to the ♡ Q. It's the very devil. I simply must ruff one of those diamonds. The first? Certainly not, for then you would throw a spade and I get only my two trump honours. I know what I'll do, I'll throw a club.'

D'Artagnan ruffed with the ♡ 5, played the ♣ 2 to the ace, then the ◇ 10 as had been foreseen.

'Now I will ruff with the ♡ J, draw the ♡ K and then, goodbye to 5 ♡,' de Busigny muttered.

'Not so fast now,' d'Artagnan replied. 'I unblock the ♡ Q under your king—and make five tricks.'

Porthos rose so quickly from his chair that it crashed down behind him. When everything had quieted down d'Artagnan said:

'Look, if you will bet a dozen bottles against *me* just for a change I shall nevertheless set 5 ♡.'

'Done!' was de Busigny's reply. 'I will follow your last plan. Where do we start?'

'We will start where you lead the ◊ 8 from dummy.' (See the foregoing diagram.)

As East d'Artagnan threw a club. De Busigny ruffed with the ♡ 5, played the ♣ 2 to the ace and continued with the ◊ 10. D'Artagnan ruffed with the ♡ J and then led the ♣ Q! This ruined the plan because later d'Artagnan could compel de Busigny to use the ♡9 on a club letting d'Artagnan make two tricks with the ♡ K and the ♡ 7!

Porthos was quite speechless, but Athos asked:

'D'Artagnan, are there any more variations?'

The reply from d'Artagnan was: 'I wonder whether M. de Busigny would like to make a fresh bet against me making five tricks?'

'No, thank you,' was the reply, 'I have lost too much already playing against you. You are a brilliant player. But please show us how.'

'With the greatest of pleasure. I ruff the ♠ A and play the ♡ 3. East covers with the ♡ 10, and is allowed to hold the trick! East leads the ♣ Q which is taken with dummy's ace, and the ♡ Q follows. East covers with the ♡ K and is again allowed to win the trick! East continues with the ♣ J to dummy's king. Then declarer finesses East's ♡ J, and when the last trump is drawn West is squeezed in spades and diamonds, and only the two trumps to East were lost.'

Everyone was again full of admiration. Rather jokingly de Busigny asked: 'And I suppose you have still another way of ruining the last plan?'

'Oh yes,' d'Artagnan replied.

'Let me try to find the weak spot,' de Busigny said. 'After winning with the ♡ 10 I will continue in trumps.'

'What trump? The 7? If you do I win with the ♡ 9 and ruff the ♠ 9. You can only get one trump trick. Or the ♡ J? Then I make six tricks by taking the trick with the queen and finessing the king. Or the ♡ K? If so I duck in the closed hand and unblock the ♡ Q from dummy.'

'But what, then, *is* the solution?' And Porthos was impatient when he said it.

'It's really all very simple,' was d'Artagnan's reply. 'On the two occasions when East is on lead he should play diamonds and not clubs. By doing that the essential entries are removed from dummy and the squeeze is killed. Indeed, only 4 ♡ can be made!'

REWARD AND PUNISHMENT

Louis XIII had become bored with the continued siege of La Rochelle and had therefore decided to return to Paris. His guard of the Musketeers escorted him there. That done the four friends obtained leave of absence so that they could search for Constance Bonacieux. The Queen had placed her in a convent for safety.

Purely by accident she had met Milady who returned from England where she had enticed Felton into the attempted murder of the Duke of Buckingham. In the convent at Béthune the musketeers found Constance at death's door from poison that Milady had somehow managed to give her. The musketeers' desire to take Milady by force was very great, particularly in the case of d'Artagnan, and Athos who had undertaken to arrange her capture had the greatest difficulty in calming the others down: he thought that the best way of relaxing would be a game of cards, and he was probably right.

South/Love all.

Porthos
♠ J 4 2
♡ 9 5
◇ Q 10 7
♣ A Q 10 9 8

D'Artagnan
♠ Q 10 7
♡ A 10 7 6 3
◇ 3 2
♣ 7 6 5

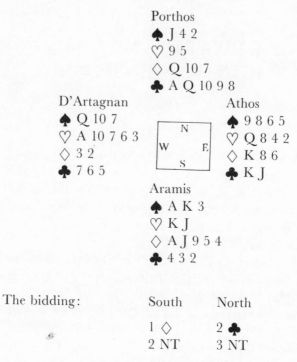

Athos
♠ 9 8 6 5
♡ Q 8 4 2
◇ K 8 6
♣ K J

Aramis
♠ A K 3
♡ K J
◇ A J 9 5 4
♣ 4 3 2

The bidding:

	South	North
	1 ◇	2 ♣
	2 NT	3 NT

D'Artagnan led the ♡ 6, and Aramis took Athos' ♡ Q with the king. He foresaw that the club finesse was dangerous as he did not hold another stopper in hearts. But, on the other hand, an unlucky diamond finesse need not lead to a direct killing because d'Artagnan could not be aware that his ♡ J was now blank. Perhaps he could try to find an entry to Athos in spades. Aramis, therefore, played a low club to the ace with the intention of finessing diamonds, but as Athos dropped the ♣ K under the ace Aramis quickly changed his mind. In the belief that d'Artagnan held the ♣ J he had no need to risk the diamond finesse, but he had his certain (?) tricks in clubs. So he played a spade to the ace, and then a club to dummy's ♣ 8.

Athos, however, who had seen through the first plan and

knew that it would succeed, now took the trick with the ♣ J, shot a heart back, and Aramis went one down.

It is unnecessary here to recall the judgement on Milady and her death—all that one need say is that she thoroughly deserved it. The moment she had landed back in France she had despatched a messenger to the Cardinal informing him of the result of her mission and deploring the way the musketeers had plotted against her. On his way back to Paris d'Artagnan had come face to face with de Rochefort, but because de Rochefort held diplomatic immunity there could be no precipitate action which would involve duelling. Cardinal de Richelieu was one of France's greatest sons whose genius was well understood by the weak Louis XIII. The King therefore supported him even against his own nearest family whose perpetual intrigues and conspiracies were inflicted on the King's favourite Cinq-Mars, as well as Montmorency and Chalais, who died on the scaffold as scapegoats.

The musketeers had, on occasion, crossed with the Cardinal, but these were mere pin-pricks compared with a conspiracy against him. In his own heart he admired the four men's courage and would have much liked to have them in his own personal service. But in the Milady affair they had gone too far, and it would seem that their lives were threatened.

It is well known that in his free time, and there was very little of that, the Cardinal was a considerable dramatist and poet, but what is not known is that he had a great interest in card problems. He had heard about the musketeers' exploits at the card table and decided he would set them a problem at bridge on which their lives would depend. This was the problem:

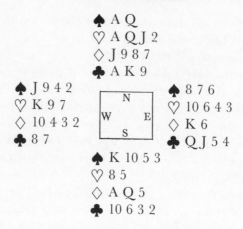

♠ A Q
♡ A Q J 2
◇ J 9 8 7
♣ A K 9

♠ J 9 4 2
♡ K 9 7
◇ 10 4 3 2
♣ 8 7

♠ 8 7 6
♡ 10 6 4 3
◇ K 6
♣ Q J 5 4

♠ K 10 5 3
♡ 8 5
◇ A Q 5
♣ 10 6 3 2

His proposition was that each of the musketeers must make a small slam in his own suit, and that finally one of them should make 6 No Trumps. The Cardinal himself would defend, and the lead should be in every case the ♠ 2.

Athos quickly saw that the club contract looked like being the most difficult with the double trump guard behind dummy's A–K, and that Porthos should be kept in reserve as long as possible for the good reason that his brain worked rather more slowly than the brains of the others. As a wise general he, therefore, said that d'Artagnan should start with the club slam—after that he himself would play 6 ◇, then Aramis 6 ♡, Porthos 6 ♠, and finally d'Artagnan would play 6 No Trumps.

D'Artagnan: 6 ♣. D'Artagnan sat down in South's place, and it didn't take him long to solve his problem. But all the same he played much slower than it was his usual custom. This was in order to give his friends a longer interval to consider their own problems, as well as to try to demonstrate to them the importance in all the contracts to go easy with the entries to South.

The contract was 6 ♣, as agreed, and West led the ♠ 2. D'Artagnan cashed the ♠ A and Q, and then played the ◇ 7 to the ◇ Q, the ♡ 5 to dummy's ♡ J, the ◇ 8 to the ace and cashed the ♠ K on which he threw dummy's ◇ 9. Then

followed a second heart finesse with the queen, and on the
♡ A d'Artagnan threw the ◇ 5! He ruffed the ♡ 2 with the
♣ 10. Now the ♣ 2 was played to dummy's king and the ◇ J
was laid down. It did not matter whether East ruffed high or
low—he could not obtain more than one trump trick, the
apparent double trump guard was halved, and d'Artagnan
had solved the difficult problem.

Athos: 6 ◇. Having to make 6 ◇ Athos did as d'Artagnan
had done and took the first three tricks with the ♠ A, the
♠ Q and the ◇ Q. But in his usual nonchalant way he dis-
dained the entries and cashed the ◇ A. Then he played the
♡ 5 to the jack, cashed the ♣ A, the ♣ K and the ♡ A,
ruffed the ♡ 2 with the ◇ 5 and cashed the ♠ K to throw
dummy's ♣ 9. He then led the ♠ 10 and let the Cardinal
hold the trick with West's ♠ J, throwing the ♡ Q from dummy
There were only two cards left, and West had to lead trumps
into dummy's tenace.

Aramis: 6 ♡. By this time it had become clear to Aramis
that with hearts as trumps he simply could not avoid to lose
a trump trick. Having cashed the ♠ A and Q he therefore
decided to lose it at once by playing the ♡ 2 from dummy.
The Cardinal won the trick with West's ♡ 7, but it would
have made no difference if he had taken it in East with the
♡ 10. He shifted to the ♣ 8 to dummy's king. Aramis first
now played the ◇ 7 to the queen and the ♡ 8 to the jack,
followed by two more rounds of trumps. With the ◇ 8 to the
ace he entered South's hand, cashed the ♠ K to throw
dummy's ♣ 9, and with a diamond finesse took the last three
tricks.

(Repeated for convenience:)

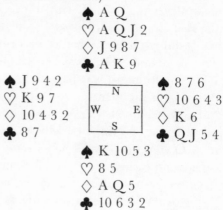

♠ A Q
♡ A Q J 2
◇ J 9 8 7
♣ A K 9

♠ J 9 4 2
♡ K 9 7
◇ 10 4 3 2
♣ 8 7

♠ 8 7 6
♡ 10 6 4 3
◇ K 6
♣ Q J 5 4

♠ K 10 5 3
♡ 8 5
◇ A Q 5
♣ 10 6 3 2

Porthos: 6 ♠. Excitement rose—could Porthos do as well as his three friends? It was natural enough for him at sometime or another to pull the wrong card, but the involuntary extravagance resulting from this increased the effect so that his play became the most elegant of all—as only Athos could play. He was to make 6 ♠, and he at once cashed dummy's two high spades and two high clubs before he played the ◇ 7 to the queen. With the ♠ K he removed East's last trump, throwing the ♣ 9 from dummy. He then took the first heart finesse with the ♡ 5 to the jack, returned to the ◇ A to take the second heart finesse with the queen. On the tenth trick he laid down the ♡ A, and here it was that he pulled the wrong card as he ruffed with the ♠ 10! He soon saw, however, that no damage was done, for he could now take two diamond tricks with a finesse, and dummy's thirteenth card, the ♡ 2, the Cardinal could take both in East and West. The three other musketeers congratulated Porthos, and even the Cardinal smiled as Porthos coolly, but proudly, accepted the compliments.

D'Artagnan: 6 No Trumps. He achieved this quickly. As earlier on he started by cashing the ♠ A–Q, played the ◇ 7 to the queen and the ♡ 5 to the jack. And then followed the decisive move—he cashed the ♡ A! The Cardinal could not unblock the ♡ K here, because the ♡ Q would then give the twelfth trick. If d'Artagnan, however, had continued playing diamonds without having made the 'Vienne Coup' in hearts the Cardinal could later on set the contract by unblocking the ♡ K under the ace. D'Artagnan now continued with three diamond tricks and then endplayed the Cardinal with the ♡ 2 to West's king. West had to give d'Artagnan the last two tricks by playing spades into the tenace.

The Cardinal, who was always appreciative of any good feat of arms and was no less so of a well-played series of games of bridge, said how satisfied he was with the musketeers' performances. The play had given him real enjoyment, and he expressed the hope that there would be more. There was, therefore, no question of any of the four men suffering injury —or even being sent to the Bastille.

INTERMEZZO

D'Artagnan, in due course, was promoted a lieutenant in the Musketeers. For some reason the actual commission was left blank, and d'Artagnan offered it in turn to each of his friends, but no one would accept it, not even the ambitious Porthos; his reason was that his cousin had become widowed and he intended to marry her and leave the service. In the end Athos filled in the commission with d'Artagnan's name, and they celebrated the occasion with a game of bridge.

North/Both.

Athos
♠ K 7 2
♡ A K 6 2
♢ A Q 5 3
♣ Q 4

Porthos
♠ A 10 5
♡ J 9 8 7
♢ K
♣ J 9 6 3 2

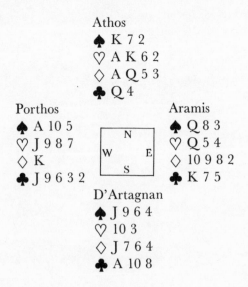

Aramis
♠ Q 8 3
♡ Q 5 4
♢ 10 9 8 2
♣ K 7 5

D'Artagnan
♠ J 9 6 4
♡ 10 3
♢ J 7 6 4
♣ A 10 8

The bidding:

North	South
1 ♡	1 ♠
3 ◇	3 NT

Porthos opened with the ♣ 3, and d'Artagnan took the king with the ace. It appeared that the only winning chance lay with Porthos holding the ◇ K doubleton and the ♠ A with the result that d'Artagnan could then get four diamond tricks and the ♠ K as the ninth trick. He played the ◇ 4— but as the king immediately appeared he was aware that this time there could be no four diamond tricks. Thus he had to try to dupe his opponents by cheekily playing spades. He had bid this suit, but he had certainly not too many entries as seen by his opponents. So when he played the ♠ K from dummy Porthos promptly ducked. Aramis saw no reason to cover the next spade and Porthos, thinking that d'Artganan also held the queen, ducked again so that the ♠ J held the trick. Having succeeded so far d'Artagnan felt no risk in trying a third spade, the ace and the queen fell together, and d'Artagnan made an overtrick!

In January, 1628, shortly before Porthos married the solicitor's widow with her dowry of 800.000 francs, he invited his friends to meet him in the suburb of Saint-Marceau. They all agreed to enter the first inn they came across, and by a curious chance it was called 'La Femme-sans-Tete'. It was only on Porthos that the name of the inn with its signboard of a headless woman made no impression—on the others there was an eerie feeling when they crossed the threshold. Porthos had completely forgotten the episode of the beheading of Milady.

East/Love all.

Athos
♠ A 3
♡ A Q 6 2
◇ A K Q 4
♣ A K 8

Aramis
♠ 2
♡ J 9 7 5
◇ J 9 8 7
♣ 10 9 4 3

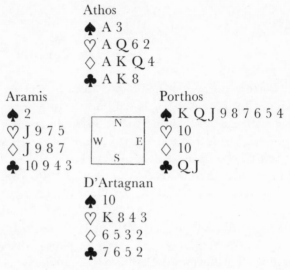

Porthos
♠ K Q J 9 8 7 6 5 4
♡ 10
◇ 10
♣ Q J

D'Artagnan
♠ 10
♡ K 8 4 3
◇ 6 5 3 2
♣ 7 6 5 2

The bidding:

East	South	West	North
4 ♠	Pass	Pass	4 NT
Pass	5 ♡		

Aramis led his singleton ♠ 2. D'Artagnan went up with dummy's ace, cashed the three high hearts and three high diamonds, and found that there was no luck with any of these suits. He then took the pleasant appearance from dummy by cashing the ♣ A–K and exited with the ♠ 3, he himself throwing his last diamond. Aramis could spare the ♣ 9. Porthos could only continue in spades, and now d'Artagnan threw the ♣ 6. What should Aramis, however, do against this so-called 'Chicker Play?' He was, in fact, squeezed in three suits, and one was the trump suit! If he ruffed with the ♡ J dummy would throw the ♣ 8, and there would be a crossruff for the remainder of the tricks. If he were to discard the ◇ J, dummy would ruff and play the ◇ 4 onto which d'Artagnan would get rid of his last club; and if Aramis were to throw the ♣ 10 it would be the ♣ 8 which would become high as d'Artagnan would ruff dummy's ◇ 4. So Aramis gave up and threw in his cards.

West/Both.

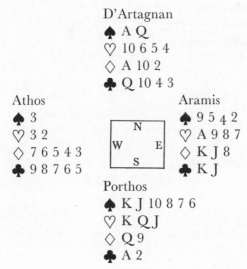

D'Artagnan
♠ A Q
♡ 10 6 5 4
◇ A 10 2
♣ Q 10 4 3

Athos
♠ 3
♡ 3 2
◇ 7 6 5 4 3
♣ 9 8 7 6 5

Aramis
♠ 9 5 4 2
♡ A 9 8 7
◇ K J 8
♣ K J

Porthos
♠ K J 10 8 7 6
♡ K Q J
◇ Q 9
♣ A 2

The bidding:

West	North	East	South
Pass	1 ♣	Dble.	2 ♠
Pass	2 NT	Pass	3 ♠
Pass	4 ♠	Pass	6 ♠

Athos led the ♡ 3. Aramis went up with the ace and returned the ♡ 9. Porthos won the trick with the ♡ Q. He played the ♠ 6 to the queen, the ♡ 6 to the king, cashed the ♣ A, and led the ♠ 7 to the ace. On dummy's ♡ 10 he threw the ♣ 2, ruffed a club and drew all the trumps. Dummy took the last two tricks with the ◇ A and the ♣ Q.

'That was a daring way to play,' d'Artagnan remarked. 'If Athos had another trump you would go down.'

'Yes,' Porthos agreed, 'but it *was* the only way to make it. And as you have seen, it worked.'

'Well, in point of fact there was at least one safer way,' d'Artagnan replied. 'You could draw six rounds of trumps and the ♡ K and keep in dummy the ♡ 10, the ◇ A and two clubs. Then you go to dummy with the ◇ A and cash the ♡ 10. Aramis has only the ◇ K and the ♣ K–J left, and you will discard after him.'

'Oh, that's too complicated,' was Porthos' answer. 'I like my own way better.'

When Porthos married in 1628 he left Paris. Aramis went on a journey to Lorraine and vanished—he did not even write to his friends. It was fairly clear that he had entered a monastery and had thus carried out his declared intention. Two duels were fought between d'Artagnan and de Rochefort and they then became reconciled. Dumas has not recorded that d'Artagnan and Athos were occasionally invited to play bridge either at the Palais-Royal or in the King's presence, and here are a few deals that were played at that particular time:

South/E–W.

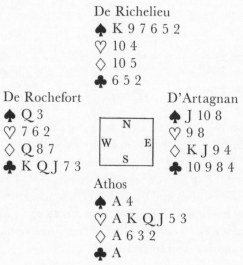

De Richelieu
♠ K 9 7 6 5 2
♡ 10 4
◇ 10 5
♣ 6 5 2

De Rochefort
♠ Q 3
♡ 7 6 2
◇ Q 8 7
♣ K Q J 7 3

D'Artagnan
♠ J 10 8
♡ 9 8
◇ K J 9 4
♣ 10 9 8 4

Athos
♠ A 4
♡ A K Q J 5 3
◇ A 6 3 2
♣ A

The bidding:

	South	North
	2 ♡	2 NT
	3 ◇	3 ♠
	6 ♡	

De Rochefort led the ♣ K. Athos took it with the ace and immediately drew three rounds of spades, ruffing the third spade with the ♡ 3! Pleased at getting a trick so cheaply with an apparently useless trump de Rochefort, without thinking, overruffed with the ♡ 6, and led the ♣ Q. Athos had seen the only possibility, and that was that de Rochefort held the doubleton ♠ Q and three trumps, and that he could not resist the temptation of winning a cheap trick with an overruff. Now Athos was in the position to draw all the outstanding trumps in two rounds, ending in dummy on the ♡ 10 so that he could rid himself of three losing diamonds on the high spades. This would not have been possible if de Rochefort had resisted the overruff.

South/Both.

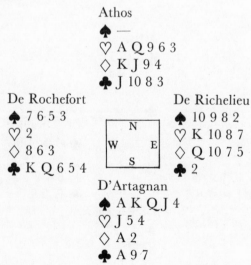

Athos
♠ —
♡ A Q 9 6 3
◇ K J 9 4
♣ J 10 8 3

De Rochefort
♠ 7 6 5 3
♡ 2
◇ 8 6 3
♣ K Q 6 5 4

De Richelieu
♠ 10 9 8 2
♡ K 10 8 7
◇ Q 10 7 5
♣ 2

D'Artagnan
♠ A K Q J 4
♡ J 5 4
◇ A 2
♣ A 9 7

The bidding:

South	North
1 ♠	2 ♡
2 NT	3 ◇
4 NT	5 ◇
5 NT	6 ◇
6 NT	

De Rochefort was most unlucky in choosing the ♣ K for his opening lead. D'Artagnan won with the ace, and continued with the ♣ 9. De Rochefort went up with the Queen, and de Richelieu seized the opportunity to echo with the ♡ 8 whereupon de Rochefort shifted to the ♡ 2. D'Artagnan resisted the temptation to finesse. Instead he went right up with the ♡ A, cashed dummy's two high clubs, and entered the closed hand with the ◇ A to run the spades. As the suit broke the Cardinal ran into difficulties on the fifth spade. He was shrewd enough to blank the ◇ Q, but in the next trick d'Artagnan played the ◇ 2 to the king and then took the last trick with the ◇ J.

East/E–W.

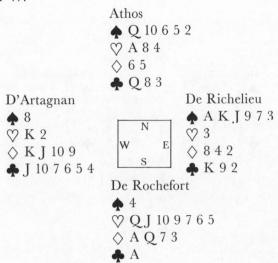

```
                        Athos
                        ♠ Q 10 6 5 2
                        ♡ A 8 4
                        ◇ 6 5
                        ♣ Q 8 3
        D'Artagnan                      De Richelieu
        ♠ 8                             ♠ A K J 9 7 3
        ♡ K 2               N           ♡ 3
        ◇ K J 10 9     W        E       ◇ 8 4 2
        ♣ J 10 7 6 5 4      S           ♣ K 9 2
                        De Rochefort
                        ♠ 4
                        ♡ Q J 10 9 7 6 5
                        ◇ A Q 7 3
                        ♣ A
```

The bidding: East   South

1 ♠   4 ♡

Apparently this contract could only be lost on the floor—but first look at d'Artagnan's defence. He led his singleton ♠ 8. The Cardinal took the trick with the ♠ 9 and continued with the ♠ A. De Rochefort ruffed with the ♡ 5, and d'Artagnan threw the ♣ 4!! Naturally enough de Rochefort was led to believe that the Cardinal held the ♡ K, and when he led the ♡ Q and d'Artagnan followed with the ♡ 2 he consequently went up with the ace. He hoped that the king had been a singleton—but even this was unnecessary, not even if the diamond finesse lost, as d'Artagnan could not lead trumps with the result that there was always time to ruff two diamond losers.

Having won with dummy's ♡ A de Rochefort led a diamond to the queen, but d'Artagnan took it with the ◇ K and cashed the ♡ K, the card he 'could not possess'. The result was that de Rochefort could only ruff one diamond, and so he went one down.

The Cardinal had mentioned to Louis XIII the two musketeers' bridge playing abilities, with the result that the King had expressed his wish to play a game with them.

South/Love all.

Athos
♠ 9 4 2
♡ K J 9 5 2
♢ Q 10
♣ A K 4

The Cardinal
♠ A
♡ 8 6 3
♢ J 9 7 3 2
♣ Q J 10 8

The King
♠ 8 3
♡ 10 7
♢ A 8 5
♣ 9 7 6 5 3 2

D'Artagnan
♠ K Q J 10 7 6 5
♡ A Q 4
♢ K 6 4
♣ —

The bidding:	South	North
	1 ♠	2 NT
	6 ♠	

The Cardinal opened with the ♣ Q. D'Artagnan thought at first that dummy's ♣ A–K were worth nothing to him, but after a moment's concentration he saw his chance. He cashed both the high clubs and discarded the ♡ 4 and the ♡ Q. Then he led a trump.

The Cardinal, winning with the ♠ A, thought that d'Artagnan did not hold any more hearts, but that he might very well be holding a losing diamond besides the ace if he were to open the suit himeslf. So he continued with the ♣ J. D'Artagnan ruffed, cashed the ♠ Q and the ♡ A and entered dummy on the ♠ 9 to throw three diamonds on the high hearts.

The King was a little angry that the Cardinal had not seen through d'Artagnan's trap, but even he had to admit that it was well sprung.

TWENTY
YEARS AFTER

Twenty years had gone by, and in all that long time d'Artagnan had lost touch with his three friends. Louis XIII and Cardinal de Richelieu had died, Louis XIV was in his minority, and Queen Anne was acting as Regent under the domination of the Italian Cardinal Mazarin. Mazarin was most unpopular with the French and the revolt of the Fronde broke out.

Mazarin had heard about d'Artagnan's earlier exploits and suggested to him that he should seek out his friends. He did ultimately find them, but only Porthos was prepared to rejoin the Musketeers—his hope being that he would be given a peerage for his services. His wealth was not enough to satisfy him; he wanted a Barony to go with it. Neither Athos nor Aramis would have any dealings with Mazarin. Indeed, after the escape by the Duc de Beaufort from Vincennes (aided by Athos' servant Grimaud) d'Artagnan then realised that they were in the opposing camp. Although the real names and titles of the three ex-musketeers are known to us it is preferable to use their pseudonyms.

It was particularly painful for Athos and d'Artagnan to be opposed to each other, but it was on Athos' inititative that politics were not allowed to disturb their old friendship. This was, indeed, renewed on a Wednesday at the inn 'L'Hermitage' in the rue de la Monnaie. Spirits were low at first, but when the wise Athos ordered champagne the atmosphere changed. Aramis loosened a too tight throat-button and Porthos at once unbuttoned his whole coat. Very soon everything was

as it was in the good old days, and in the subsequent game of
bridge d'Artagnan was able to show that he had lost none of
his old skill.

East/Love all.

Athos
♠ 5 4
♡ J 8 4 3
◇ 7 6
♣ Q 9 8 6 3

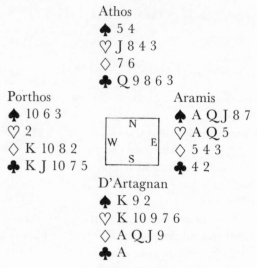

Porthos
♠ 10 6 3
♡ 2
◇ K 10 8 2
♣ K J 10 7 5

Aramis
♠ A Q J 8 7
♡ A Q 5
◇ 5 4 3
♣ 4 2

D'Artagnan
♠ K 9 2
♡ K 10 9 7 6
◇ A Q J 9
♣ A

The bidding:

East	South	West	North
1 ♠	Dble.	2 ♣	Pass
2 ♠	3 ♡	Pass	4 ♡
Dble.			

Indeed, in their first deal when Athos raised to 4 ♡ he
showed his great confidence in d'Artagnan's expertise.

Porthos led the ♠ 10 which Aramis took with the ace to
shift to the ♣ 4. D'Artagnan won with the ace, cashed the
♠ K and ruffed the third spade to try the diamond finesse,
which, however, went to Porthos' king. Expecting Aramis to
have a singleton Porthos played the ♣ K, and this gave
d'Artagnan the chance of a very rare endplay. He ruffed,
cashed the ◇ A and ruffed the ◇ 9. He then played the ♡ 8

from dummy. But Aramis was too shrewd to duck; he went
up with the ace, and the situation was:

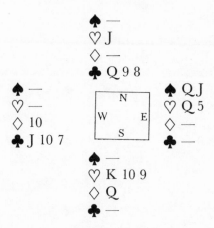

Again, Aramis was too shrewd to play a trump. Instead he
played a spade for a ruff and discard, but it didn't help him.
D'Artagnan ruffed with the ♡ 9 and overruffed with
dummy's ♡ J! When the ♣ Q followed from dummy
Aramis was helpless. He threw the last spade, but d'Artagnan
having rid himself of the trump he had too many could
now stay in dummy by throwing the ◊ Q, and in the two
last cards he held a tenace over Aramis' trumps. To
d'Artagnan, who had not looked particularly pleased when
Athos put the dummy down, Athos said:

'There you are. Why stop at 3 ♡ when four are cold?'

Obviously, the renewal of their close friendship gave the
four men much pleasure, and Aramis' sometimes slippery
tactics went without criticism; indeed, the three others
laughed and joked about the fact that he never seemed able
to change his ways.

South/Love all.

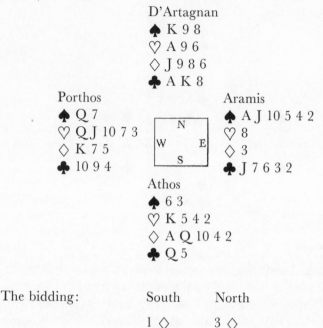

D'Artagnan
♠ K 9 8
♡ A 9 6
◇ J 9 8 6
♣ A K 8

Porthos
♠ Q 7
♡ Q J 10 7 3
◇ K 7 5
♣ 10 9 4

Aramis
♠ A J 10 5 4 2
♡ 8
◇ 3
♣ J 7 6 3 2

Athos
♠ 6 3
♡ K 5 4 2
◇ A Q 10 4 2
♣ Q 5

The bidding:

	South	North
	1 ◇	3 ◇
	3 NT	

Porthos led the ♡ Q which was taken with dummy's ace, and Athos followed with the ♡ 5 in order to make Aramis' ♡ 8 look as it if were an echo. Athos played the ◇ J from dummy, and Aramis dropped the ♣ 2.

'No diamonds, Aramis?' Porthos asked.

'I'm sorry! Aramis replied. 'I thought that hearts were played.' He picked up the ♣ 2 and followed with the ◇ 3.

As Aramis had admitted that he held no more hearts and was not interested in clubs, spades were the only chance. After winning with the ◇ K Porthos, therefore, shifted to the ♠ Q; Aramis took six spade tricks and the contract went three down.

East/N–S.

D'Artagnan
♠ J 5
♡ K 10
♢ A 9 8 5 2
♣ K J 8 5

Aramis
♠ K 4 2
♡ 5 4 2
♢ K Q 6 4
♣ 9 4 2

Porthos
♠ A Q 9 6 3
♡ A 8
♢ J 7 3
♣ 10 7 3

Athos
♠ 10 8 7
♡ Q J 9 7 6 3
♢ 10
♣ A Q 6

The bidding:

East	South	West	North
1 ♠	2 ♡	2 ♠	3 ♢
Pass	3 ♡	Pass	4 ♡

Aramis opened with the ♠ 2. Porthos went up with the ace, drew the ♡ A and continued with the ♡ 8. Athos played a club to the ace, drew the last trump, then shifted back to clubs and discarded one of his spade losers on the fourth club.

'If I don't play trumps he can ruff a spade,' Porthos commented.

'True,' d'Artagnan replied. 'But you should have shifted to the ♡ 8 and not the ace. If Athos had then tried to get a ruff one of you wins and continues trumps, and then you would be in a winning position. You would be on lead with the ♡ A and could cash the third spade. Or, should Athos play four rounds of clubs. Aramis could ruff with a low trump and in doing that the contract would be set.'

Mazarin, who had picked up the story of the diamond

studs during the reign of Louis XIII, decided that one
evening he would bring Porthos and d'Artagnan along with
him to the Queen's game of bridge. He was curious to see how
the Queen would react. In that he was disappointed, for she
showed no emotion and had apparently forgotten the whole
affair.

South/N–S.

D'Artagnan
♠ J 8
♡ A Q 9 7 4
◇ K Q 7
♣ 8 5 2

Mazarin
♠ A 10 9 6 5 3
♡ 5 2
◇ J 9 4
♣ 6 3

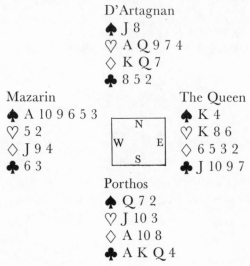

The Queen
♠ K 4
♡ K 8 6
◇ 6 5 3 2
♣ J 10 9 7

Porthos
♠ Q 7 2
♡ J 10 3
◇ A 10 8
♣ A K Q 4

The bidding:

South	West	North	East
1 ♣	1 ♠	2 ♡	Pass
2 NT	Pass	3 NT	

Mazarin opened with the ♠ 10, and the ♠ 8 was played
from dummy. The Queen intended to go up with the king,
but her mind was distracted by the young Louis XIV, and
she dropped the ♠ 4. Porthos let fall the ♠ 7, but just caught
it, playing, and winning with the ♠ Q. But the Queen
protested and demanded that he should play the ♠ 7.
Mazarin gave her foot a gentle pressure and said:

'Mon Dieu, Madame, let us be understanding and not treat your guests with too much severity.'

The Queen had never seen such humanity in Mazarin, even when playing cards, but she followed his advice and gave in. D'Artagnan was unable to do anything. Porthos thus won the trick with the ♠ Q and played the ♡ J letting it ride to the Queen's ♡ K. She played the ♠ K which Mazarin could now afford to take over with the ace and to cash four more spade tricks. Porthos went two down.

D'Artagnan hadn't the heart to tell Porthos what a famous coup he could have made by ducking with the ♠ 7 to the first trick.

Mazarin ordered d'Artagnan and Porthos to go to England with a message from him to Cromwell, and instructions to place themselves at the latter's disposal while they were there. Consequently they took part in the battle in which Charles I was made prisoner. It was here they again met up with Athos and Aramis on the opposing side. They pretended to take them prisoners and to guard their 'prisoners' themselves, escorting them to their lodging-house in Newcastle, and intending to follow the captured King's escort to London. Athos' hope was still to save the King, but when Aramis asked him what his plans were he admitted he did not know but felt sure that d'Artagnan would find some sort of plan.

Having exchanged reminiscences about their several exploits they dealt the cards and played the following hand before they were interrupted by Mordaunt:

South/Love all.

D'Artagnan
♠ 6
♡ A 6 5 2
◇ 10 5 4
♣ A 8 6 4 2

Porthos
♠ 8 7 4
♡ K 9 4
◇ J 7 3
♣ J 7 5 3

Aramis
♠ K Q J 9 5 3
♡ J 10 8 3
◇ Q
♣ K 9

Athos
♠ A 10 2
♡ Q 7
◇ A K 9 8 6 2
♣ Q 10

The bidding:

South	West	North	East
1 ◇	Pass	2 ♣	2 ♠
2 NT	Pass	3 ♣	3 ♠
3 NT			

Porthos led the ♠ 8, and Athos quickly won with the ace. He then led the ◇ A, and when the queen dropped he continued, without any hesitation, with the ◇ 2. Porthos swallowed the bait. In the belief that Aramis held the single-ton king he ducked with the ◇ 7, and so Athos made the six diamond tricks that he needed for the contract.

It was at this point that the game was interrupted by Mordaunt. He was Milady's son and had somehow learned that the cause of her death was his uncle, Lord Winter, together with four French noblemen. Moreover he had guessed that Athos and Aramis were two of the latter, but he had no idea that the messengers sent by Mazarin to Cromwell were the other two. With Cromwell's permission he came to take charge of the 'prisoners', but d'Artagnan insisted on having a written request together with a considerable sum in ransom money. Very angry, Mordaunt had to agree to d'Artagnan's demands and left to see whether they could be fulfilled. After he had gone the four re-united friends fought through the soldiers left by Mordaunt, d'Artagnan's idea being to follow and join the escort of the royal prisoner to London. It would be believed by everyone, so he thought, that the fugitives had gone in the opposite direction.

At their first resting-place they took advantage of the rare opportunity to have a game of bridge, and it was here that Athos accomplished this 'Coup de Luxe':

South/Love all.

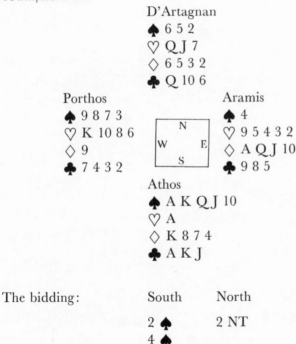

D'Artagnan
♠ 6 5 2
♡ Q J 7
♢ 6 5 3 2
♣ Q 10 6

Porthos
♠ 9 8 7 3
♡ K 10 8 6
♢ 9
♣ 7 4 3 2

Aramis
♠ 4
♡ 9 5 4 3 2
♢ A Q J 10
♣ 9 8 5

Athos
♠ A K Q J 10
♡ A
♢ K 8 7 4
♣ A K J

The bidding:

	South	North
	2 ♠	2 NT
	4 ♠	

Porthos led his singleton ♢ 9. Aramis went up with the ace and continued with the ♢ Q. Athos had to cover with the

king which was ruffed by Porthos, who then shifted to the
♠ 7. Athos drew the last two trumps and then the ♡ A and
the ♣ A. He then took the ♣ J over with dummy's ♣ Q so
that he could play the ♡ Q and unblock the ♣ K from the
closed hand. Porthos won with the ♡ K, but had to play a
heart or a club to dummy, and thus Athos got rid of his two
diamond losers.

Porthos could, of course, have ducked the ♡ Q, but if he
had done so Athos would have thrown one of the diamonds
on the ♣ 10.

It was not so very long before d'Artagnan was able to
show that he had not lost his old skill.

North/N–S.

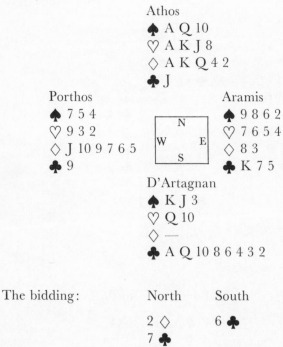

Athos
♠ A Q 10
♡ A K J 8
◇ A K Q 4 2
♣ J

Porthos
♠ 7 5 4
♡ 9 3 2
◇ J 10 9 7 6 5
♣ 9

Aramis
♠ 9 8 6 2
♡ 7 6 5 4
◇ 8 3
♣ K 7 5

D'Artagnan
♠ K J 3
♡ Q 10
◇ —
♣ A Q 10 8 6 4 3 2

The bidding:

North	South
2 ◇	6 ♣
7 ♣	

Porthos led the ◇ J. This was the only suit that would give
d'Artagnan a chance to make the grand slam, because this

gave him an extra ruffing possibility. He had it clearly in his mind that he could not rely upon the ♣ K being a singleton or doubleton, but now he would be able to stand up to Aramis having it third. So he covered the lead with dummy's ♦ Q, but ruffed with the ♣ 2. He took the ♥ Q over with dummy's king to lead the ♣ J. It held the trick, and Porthos' ♣ 9 confirmed his foreboding. The ♦ K was ruffed with the ♣ 4, the ♥ 10 taken over with the ♥ J, and now the ♦ A was ruffed with the ♣ 6. Aramis discarded a spade, but as he held four of them he had to follow suit on the three occasions d'Artagnan entered dummy in spades—the first two occasions to ruff the ♥ A and the ♥ 8 and the last to be in dummy with only two cards left and the tenace over East's trumps. A *five-double* 'Grand Coup'.

On the following day they caught up with the King and his escort. In the escort was a certain Captain Groslow with whom d'Artagnan and Porthos had already become acquainted in Cromwell's camp. Groslow, in civilian life, had been a slaughterer and Porthos nick-named him 'Manslaughter'. They were able to renew their acquaintance over cards, and as Groslow was to be on guard over the King in his rooms on the third night it was agreed that that night's game, which he wouldn't miss on any account, was to be played there. It was the intention to abduct the King that night. The evening came and, once again, Athos' confidence in d'Artagnan was proven.

North/Both.

Athos
♠ K Q 3 2
♡ A 8 2
◇ A 9
♣ A 8 4 3

Groslow
♠ J 10 9 4
♡ K 7 5 3
◇ 10 5
♣ K Q J

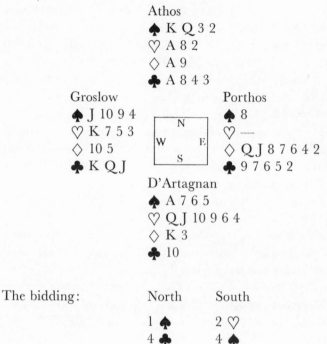

Porthos
♠ 8
♡ —
◇ Q J 8 7 6 4 2
♣ 9 7 6 5 2

D'Artagnan
♠ A 7 6 5
♡ Q J 10 9 6 4
◇ K 3
♣ 10

The bidding:

	North	South
	1 ♠	2 ♡
	4 ♣	4 ♠
	6 ♡	

Groslow opened with the ♣ K. D'Artagnan won with dummy's ace, ruffed the ♣ 3 and played the ♡ Q. As it held the trick he continued with the ♡ J, which also held. Porthos' void seemed unlucky. But d'Artagnan did not give up and said equivocally: 'Watch your king, Captain.'

'If you mean the trump king,' Groslow replied with a loud laugh, 'it is just as well guarded as Charles Stuart. You cannot draw the trump king with your blank ace.'

'Don't be so sure,' was d'Artagnan's answer. And he now rapidly cashed the ◇ A–K and the ♠ A–K, showing that Groslow too, held a spade stopper. Then he ruffed a club with the ♡ 6 and entered dummy with the ♠ Q. There were now only three cards left:

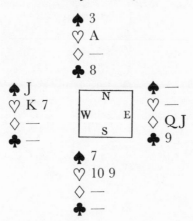

D'Artagnan played the ♣ 8 from dummy and let Porthos hold the trick with the ♣ 9, throwing the ♠ 7 from the closed hand! When Porthos had now to play a diamond Groslow's ♡ K was lost. If he covered the ♡ 9 with the king it would be taken with dummy's ace, and if he ducked with the ♡ 7 dummy would throw the ♠ 3 and take the last trick with the ♡ A.

'What a devilish coup!' exclaimed Groslow.

'Yes,' agreed Aramis, who was kibitzing, 'let's call it "Le Coup du Diable"!'

It was not due to any fault on the part of d'Artagnan that the rescue of Charles I was not accomplished that night. When the attempt was going to be made their game had been interrupted by Mordaunt who had brought instructions with regard to the royal prisoner. The four musketeers had to fight their way out and flee again—without the King. Feeling sure that they would now try to get back to France Mordaunt instituted a search at all seaports. He was mistaken; they went by unfrequented roads to London where they stayed at the 'Bedford Tavern' in Greenhall Street. They would, in due course, make another attempt at rescuing the King, and in the meantime, to soothe their nerves, they played cards.

South/Both.   D'Artagnan
                              ♠ 4
                              ♡ K 9 4 2
                              ◇ 6 3
                              ♣ A K Q 9 7 6

Porthos   Aramis
♠ A K 9 6 3   ♠ 10 8 5 2
♡ 7   ♡ Q 6 3
◇ Q 9 7 4   ◇ 10 8 5
♣ 8 5 2   ♣ J 4 3

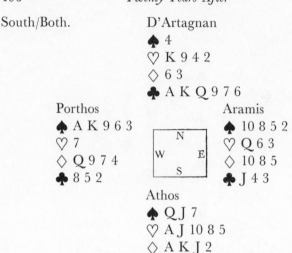

                              Athos
                              ♠ Q J 7
                              ♡ A J 10 8 5
                              ◇ A K J 2
                              ♣ 10

The bidding:

South	West	North	East
1 ♡	1 ♠	2 ♣	Pass
2 ◇	Pass	3 ♡	Pass
3 ♠	Pass	4 ♣	Pass
6 ♡			

At the same time as he passed Aramis pulled the ♡ 6 from
his hand as if to lead it. It was done in such a way that only
Athos could have noticed it—certainly not Porthos. But Athos
at once said that it was Porthos to lead. It would never have
been cleared up what Athos would have done if he had had
himself to seek after the ♡ Q, for in the first place it was quite
crazy to lead a trump from the queen. But, on the other hand,
Athos knew Aramis through and through and was well aware
that Aramis had never in the past led out of turn.

It was then that Porthos chose the very worst lead possible,
opening with his singleton trump, and folllowing that Athos
could soon claim all thirteen tricks. And Aramis' attempted
trickery on this occasion scored no points.

North/Both.

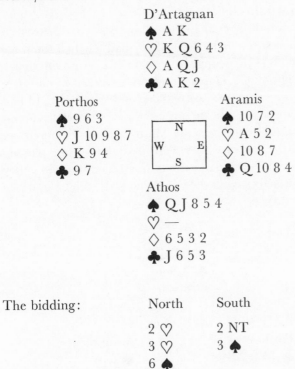

D'Artagnan
♠ A K
♡ K Q 6 4 3
◇ A Q J
♣ A K 2

Porthos
♠ 9 6 3
♡ J 10 9 8 7
◇ K 9 4
♣ 9 7

Aramis
♠ 10 7 2
♡ A 5 2
◇ 10 8 7
♣ Q 10 8 4

Athos
♠ Q J 8 5 4
♡ —
◇ 6 5 3 2
♣ J 6 5 3

The bidding:

North	South
2 ♡	2 NT
3 ♡	3 ♠
6 ♠	

Porthos led the ♡ J, covered with the queen and ace, and ruffed by Athos. If the hand was played with care it would not offer any particular difficulties, for only a club trick would have to be lost. But Athos never liked following a beaten path, and this is the amusing and original way he chose to play:

Winning the first trick with the ♠ 4 he immediately played the ◇ 2 to dummy's ◇ J, cashed the ♠ A–K and the ♡ K on which he threw the ♣ 3, ruffed a heart with the ♠ J and drew the ♠ Q on which he jettisoned dummy's ♣ A! Another diamond finesse and the ◇ A established the ◇ 6, and he now played dummy's ♣ K and continued with the ♣ 2. Aramis tried to make it difficult by playing the ♣ 8, but

Athos went up with ♣ J, cashed the ◇ 6, and lost the last trick to Aramis in clubs.

History cannot be changed by allowing the musketeers to achieve the rescue of Charles I. They had reached the stage when they were now fugitives on board a fishing smack named 'Lightning'. Dumas must, however, be mistaken when he wrote that they were asleep and that Grimaud had to awaken them when he discovered that the vessel was about to be blown up by their enemy Mordaunt who had crept on board. On the contrary they were passing the time playing bridge, and when Grimaud came to tell them the news they had just finished playing the following deals which should be put on record:

South/Love all.

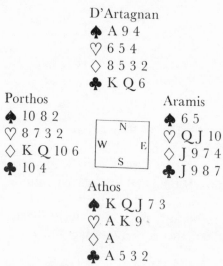

D'Artagnan
♠ A 9 4
♡ 6 5 4
◇ 8 5 3 2
♣ K Q 6

Porthos
♠ 10 8 2
♡ 8 7 3 2
◇ K Q 10 6
♣ 10 4

Aramis
♠ 6 5
♡ Q J 10
◇ J 9 7 4
♣ J 9 8 7

Athos
♠ K Q J 7 3
♡ A K 9
◇ A
♣ A 5 3 2

The bidding:

	South	North
	1 ♠	2 ♣
	4 ♣	4 ♠
	6 ♠	

Porthos opened with the ◇ K and Athos won with the ace. It was then already clear that the best chance would be to draw two rounds of trumps, and then try the clubs. This would give the following possibilities: Club distribution 3–3; club distribution 4–2 with the two in the East hand; club distribution 4–2 with the long club together with the last trump.

As has been pointed out Athos was never afraid of giving his opponents a chance. He could certainly not know that none of the above-mentioned possibilities would work this time, but that on the contrary the very imaginative method he chose was the only solution.

To the second trick he played the ♣ 2 to the queen to ruff the ◇ 3 with the ♠ K. Then he played the ♣ 3 to the ♣ K to ruff the ◇ 5 with the ♠ Q. Then he made the so-called 'unnecessary' finesse with the ♠ 9 to ruff the last diamond with the ♠ J, and finally the ♠ 7 to the ace. And now here Athos was at his most imaginative—he played the ♠ 4 from dummy, and endplayed Porthos on the ♠ 10. Aramis had up to now been able to follow to anything but on this trump lead he came into difficulties. He decided to discard a club whereupon Athos threw the ♡ 9—and took the rest of the tricks.

This was a complicated playing-plan which today we would call a dummy reversal with an 'unnecessary' finesse and endplay with a suicide squeeze.

D'Artagnan was struck dumb with admiration, and could only bow in homage to a partner who equalled him in strength of imagination.

South/N–S.

D'Artagnan
♠ 5 2
♡ 9 5 4 2
◇ Q J 9
♣ 10 9 3 2

Porthos
♠ K 10 8
♡ K Q 10 7
◇ 7 4 3 2
♣ 7 4

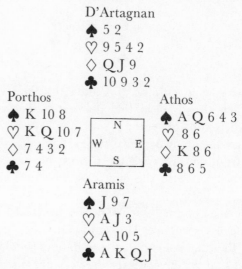

Athos
♠ A Q 6 4 3
♡ 8 6
◇ K 8 6
♣ 8 6 5

Aramis
♠ J 9 7
♡ A J 3
◇ A 10 5
♣ A K Q J

The auction could not have been shorter, with Aramis
bidding 3 No Trumps. As Porthos was West perhaps he
counted on a favourable lead. Perfectly naturally Porthos
led the ♡ K, and Aramis dropped the ♡ J! With this quite
ethical 'Coup de l'Arsenic', itself a devilish variety of the
'Bath Coup', he tempted Porthos, believing that the ace was
now singleton, to continue with the ♡ 7. The coup succeeded.
Dummy got an entry on the ♡ 9, giving not only an extra
heart trick but also the possibility of the diamond finesse—
and nine tricks in all.

South/Both.

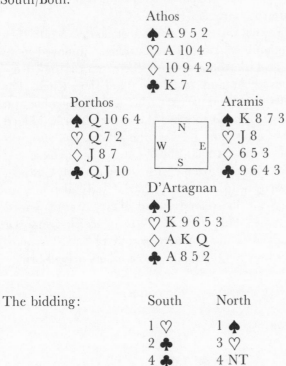

Athos
♠ A 9 5 2
♡ A 10 4
◇ 10 9 4 2
♣ K 7

Porthos
♠ Q 10 6 4
♡ Q 7 2
◇ J 8 7
♣ Q J 10

Aramis
♠ K 8 7 3
♡ J 8
◇ 6 5 3
♣ 9 6 4 3

D'Artagnan
♠ J
♡ K 9 6 5 3
◇ A K Q
♣ A 8 5 2

The bidding:

South	North
1 ♡	1 ♠
2 ♣	3 ♡
4 ♣	4 NT
7 ♡	

Porthos opened with the ♣ Q. D'Artagnan won with the ace and saw at once that unless the ♡ Q–J were doubleton he probably had to lose a trump trick. But not relying on this he did not draw trumps. Instead he played the ♠ J to the ace and ruffed a spade with the ♡ 3, then the ♣ 2 to the king to ruff another spade with the ♡ 5. The ♣ 5 was ruffed with dummy's ♡ 4 in order to ruff the last spade with the ♡ 6. After cashing the three high diamonds d'Artagnan finally played the ♣ 8 and ruffed it with dummy's ♡ 10. As East had to follow, the two high trumps took the two last tricks. If Porthos had ruffed the ♣ 8 with the ♡ Q, d'Artagnan would have taken it with the ♡ A, and then finessed the ♡ J through Aramis, expecting split honours.

Thus the opponents' apparently certain trump trick disappeared into thin air.

Because of their disregard of his instructions while they were in England Mazarin was extremely annoyed with d'Artagnan and Porthos, and on their return they were placed under arrest and taken to the Palais Rueil. For reasons of safety they had parted earlier from both Athos and Aramis, but when the former heard of their arrest he lodged a protest, and for his pains he was arrested too. He, also, was taken to the Palais Rueil. But the three men were too formidable for Mazarin to cope with—they not only escaped, but also managed to kidnap Mazarin and take him to Porthos' Chateau Pierrefonds. And there Aramis joined forces with them. They treated Mazarin as an honoured guest and, indeed, while d'Artagnan rode to Saint-Germain to intercede with the Queen, the three others played bridge with him.

The following are some of the hands:

South/Love all.

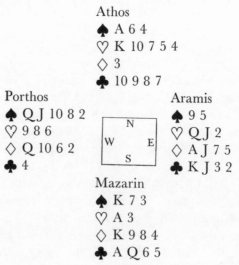

Athos
♠ A 6 4
♡ K 10 7 5 4
◇ 3
♣ 10 9 8 7

Porthos
♠ Q J 10 8 2
♡ 9 8 6
◇ Q 10 6 2
♣ 4

Aramis
♠ 9 5
♡ Q J 2
◇ A J 7 5
♣ K J 3 2

Mazarin
♠ K 7 3
♡ A 3
◇ K 9 8 4
♣ A Q 6 5

The bidding:

	South	North
	1 ♣	1 ♡
	1 NT	3 ♣
	5 ♣	

Porthos led the ♠ Q which Mazarin took with dummy's ace to lead the ◇ 3. Aramis went up with the ace to continue with the ♠ 9. Mazarin won with the ♠ K, cashed the ◇ K to throw dummy's last spade, and then he led the ♠ 7. And now the very shrewd Mazarin was fooled by the no less shrewd Aramis who overruffed dummy's ♣ 7—with the ♣ K! It was only reasonable for Mazarin now to believe that Porthos held the ♣ J. When Aramis shifted to the ♡ J Mazarin consequently took it with the ace, and drew two rounds of clubs from the top. He looked most disconcerted when he had to lose the ♣ J to Aramis. It was a very clever defence to overruff with the king and thereby 'deny' the possession of the jack. Had he overruffed with the ♣ J Mazarin would automatically have tried to finesse the ♣ K through Aramis, and successfully.

North/Love all.

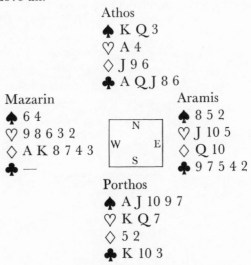

Athos
♠ K Q 3
♡ A 4
◇ J 9 6
♣ A Q J 8 6

Mazarin
♠ 6 4
♡ 9 8 6 3 2
◇ A K 8 7 4 3
♣ —

Aramis
♠ 8 5 2
♡ J 10 5
◇ Q 10
♣ 9 7 5 4 2

Porthos
♠ A J 10 9 7
♡ K Q 7
◇ 5 2
♣ K 10 3

The bidding:

North	East	South	West
1 ♣	Pass	1 ♠	2 ◇
2 ♠	Pass	4 ♠	

Instead of passing when his turn came Aramis led the ◇ Q. Porthos pointed out that it was not his lead, and Mazarin asked Porthos whether he would treat the ◇ Q as a penalty card or whether he wanted another suit led. After all, this was more than three hundred years ago with the old rules— still in force forty years ago—permitting a declarer to have these alternative choices.

Porthos, in the belief that Athos' club suit might lack the queen, then asked for a club lead. But instead Mazarin led the ◇ 3! This made it clear, of course, that he had no clubs and consequently could lead what he chose to. With dummy's ◇ 9 Porthos tried to force the queen from Aramis, but he won with the ◇ 10! He shifted to a club which Mazarin ruffed and was put on lead again with a low diamond to the ◇ Q to give Mazarin another club ruff. Thus, by their stealth the cunning Italian and the wily student of the Jesuits succeeded in setting an apparently ice-cold contract.

South/Love all.

Aramis
♠ K 9 8 7 4
♡ 10 8
◇ 10 9 5 2
♣ Q 9

Porthos
♠ J 6 3
♡ J 7
◇ A J 7
♣ K J 7 3 2

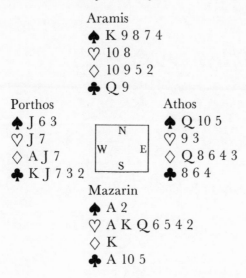

Athos
♠ Q 10 5
♡ 9 3
◇ Q 8 6 4 3
♣ 8 6 4

Mazarin
♠ A 2
♡ A K Q 6 5 4 2
◇ K
♣ A 10 5

After a good many bids Porthos opened with the ♡ J against the contract 6 ♡. Mazarin won with the ♡ A, played three rounds of spades, ruffing the third, entered dummy with a low heart to the ♡ 10, and got rid of two of his three losers on the two good spades. It was, of course, a very unlucky lead, but the tragi-comedy of it was that Porthos should not have led at all. Mazarin had agreed with Aramis to play an artificial Italian system of short-suit bidding— Mazarin opening with 1 ◇ and Aramis responding with 1 ♡, so that the final contract of 6 ♡ should really have been played by North.

South/Love all.

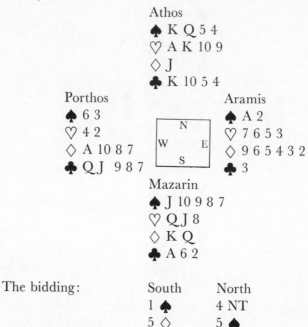

                           Athos
                           ♠ K Q 5 4
                           ♡ A K 10 9
                           ◇ J
                           ♣ K 10 5 4

        Porthos   Aramis
        ♠ 6 3   ♠ A 2
        ♡ 4 2   ♡ 7 6 5 3
        ◇ A 10 8 7   ◇ 9 6 5 4 3 2
        ♣ Q J 9 8 7   ♣ 3

                           Mazarin
                           ♠ J 10 9 8 7
                           ♡ Q J 8
                           ◇ K Q
                           ♣ A 6 2

The bidding: South   North
                        1 ♠   4 NT
                        5 ◇   5 ♠

Porthos led the ♣ Q which Mazarin took with the ace in
the closed hand. Before he could play a card to the next trick
Aramis told him that he had to confess that Monsieur du
Vallon (Porthos) had quite involuntarily shown him the ♣ J.

Mazarin was not the sort of person to give anything away.
He praised Aramis for his honesty, but demanded that the
♣ J should be placed on the table as a penalty card. In fact,
Aramis had not seen any card at all but, of course, everyone
knew that Porthos must be holding the ♣ J if he led the ♣ Q.
Mazarin had, however, not yet learned of Aramis' underhand
practices.

Mazarin played a trump to dummy's king. Aramis took it
with the ace at once and then led a diamond to Porthos' ace
—it was evident from the bidding that Porthos held the ◇ A.
Now Porthos had to play the penalty card ♣ J, 'honest'
Aramis ruffed, and the contract went one down.

North/N–S.

Athos
♠ J
♡ Q J 10 6 4 3
◇ 9 8 7 5 3
♣ K

Aramis
♠ A 6 5 3 2
♡ 9 8 7 5
◇ —
♣ Q 5 3 2

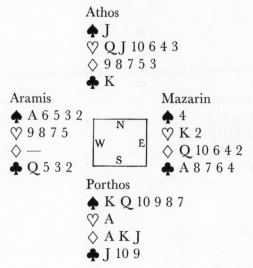

Mazarin
♠ 4
♡ K 2
◇ Q 10 6 4 2
♣ A 8 7 6 4

Porthos
♠ K Q 10 9 8 7
♡ A
◇ A K J
♣ J 10 9

The bidding:

North	East	South	West
Pass	Pass	1 ♠	Pass
2 ♡	2 NT	4 ♠	

Aramis opened with the ♣ 2. Mazarin took dummy's king with the ace and shifted to the ♠ 4. Before Porthos had even touched a card Aramis threw the ♠ 2. Porthos chose to go up with the king so as to be able to continue in trumps. Aramis won the third round, cashed the ♣ Q and continued in clubs to declarer's jack. Porthos now ran all his trumps, but Mazarin had no difficulties, for he had understood correctly Aramis' message. The too prompt discard of the ♠ 2 could only mean that Aramis had no fear of giving dummy an entry on the ♠ J to finesse hearts or diamonds. As a consequence Aramis had to be void in diamonds, and must either hold the ♡ A or be aware that Porthos held it singleton. Mazarin could therefore quietly discard his hearts and get the ◇ Q in the end.

North/N–S.

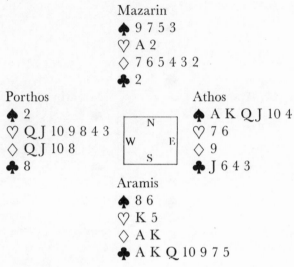

Mazarin
♠ 9 7 5 3
♡ A 2
◇ 7 6 5 4 3 2
♣ 2

Porthos
♠ 2
♡ Q J 10 9 8 4 3
◇ Q J 10 8
♣ 8

Athos
♠ A K Q J 10 4
♡ 7 6
◇ 9
♣ J 6 4 3

Aramis
♠ 8 6
♡ K 5
◇ A K
♣ A K Q 10 9 7 5

The bidding:

West	North	East	South
3 ♡	Pass	4 ♠	5 ♣

Porthos led his singleton spade. Athos won with the ♠ 10 and continued with the ♠ J which Aramis ruffed with the ♣ 9, Porthos discarding a low heart. Mazarin inquired of Aramis if he had no more spades, and after a careful look at his hand Aramis saw that he had the ♠ 8 which he exchanged for the ♣ 9. In the meantime Aramis had found out that Porthos could not overruff the ♣ 9. So he won the following trick with the ◇ A and entered dummy with the ♡ 5 to the ace in order to take the club finesse. He took the rest of the tricks.

The 'Fronde' had ended. D'Artagnan and Porthos, who had brought the Queen and the Princes, as well as Mazarin, from Paris under cover, now escorted them back again. They were invited to a game of bridge with the Queen.

East/N–S.

D'Artagnan
- ♠ 10 8 2
- ♡ 10 8
- ◇ A K J 5
- ♣ 7 4 3 2

Mazarin
- ♠ Q J
- ♡ 9 7 4 3
- ◇ 8 7 6 3
- ♣ J 10 8

The Queen
- ♠ 6 4 3
- ♡ K 6 5
- ◇ 10 9
- ♣ A K Q 9 5

Porthos
- ♠ A K 9 7 5
- ♡ A Q J 2
- ◇ Q 4 2
- ♣ 6

The bidding:

East	South	West	North
1 ♣	Dble.	Pass	2 ◇
Pass	2 ♠	Pass	3 ♠
Pass	4 ♠		

Mazarin opened with the ♣ J which the Queen took with the ♣ Q, to continue with the ♣ K. Porthos ruffed with the ♠ 7—and Mazarin threw the ◇ 3. The Queen who saw that two clubs were missing said:

'Have you no more clubs, Monsieur?'

After a little delay Mazarin found he held the ♣ 8; but he had succeeded in giving Porthos the impression that he held no trump higher than the ♠ 7. And so Porthos played the ◇ 2 to dummy's king so that he could play dummy's ♠ 10 and let it ride. Mazarin threw the ◇ 6.

'And no spades, Monsieur?'

Mazarin feigned another little search, and found the ♠ J with which he took the trick. He exited with the ◇ 6. Porthos was by now convinced that the Queen held the ♠ Q. He therefore went up with dummy's ◇ K to lead the ♠ 2 and finesse with the nine, but this time Mazarin took it at once with the ♠ Q to lead a diamond which the Queen ruffed so that the contract went one down.

Before the four friends separated for the second time (and they were not to meet again for nearly ten years) they said their 'Adieus' at the 'Hotel Grand-Roi-Charlenagne'. Dumas has stated that Athos and Aramis were dressed for travelling, but they must have changed their clothes because in Planchet's notes there are details of a couple of deals played before they left.

West/Love all.

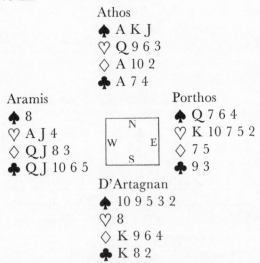

Athos
♠ A K J
♡ Q 9 6 3
◇ A 10 2
♣ A 7 4

Aramis
♠ 8
♡ A J 4
◇ Q J 8 3
♣ Q J 10 6 5

Porthos
♠ Q 7 6 4
♡ K 10 7 5 2
◇ 7 5
♣ 9 3

D'Artagnan
♠ 10 9 5 3 2
♡ 8
◇ K 9 6 4
♣ K 8 2

The bidding:

West	North	East	South
1 ♣	Dble.	Pass	1 ♠
Pass	1 NT	Pass	2 ♠
Pass	4 ♠	Dble.	

It is curious that Porthos had not become wiser with experience. It is very probable that d'Artganan could have made the contract even without the double, but Porthos should have realised that when he doubled it meant that he had almost shown his cards to a player of d'Artagnan's class.

Aramis led the ♣ Q and, in a flash, d'Artagnan saw that in addition to the ace and the king in the two minor suits he needed six trump tricks. This was indeed possible if he could, besides ruffing three hearts, endplay Porthos so that he had to play trumps into the tenace. So he took the first trick with the ♣ K and then played the ♡ 8. Porthos won the trick with the ♡ 10 and continued in clubs. D'Artagnan took it with dummy's ace and ruffed a heart. He played a trump to dummy's ace, and ruffed another heart. Then a diamond to the ace to ruff the last heart. He cashed the ◊ K for his eighth trick and exited in clubs. Aramis won and Porthos threw the ♡ K, but when Aramis cashed the ◊ Q Porthos had only trumps left. He had to ruff and to lead into the tenace in dummy.

South/N–S.

                        D'Artagnan
                        ♠ 9 8
                        ♡ A Q 8
                        ◊ 9 4 2
                        ♣ A Q 10 9 3

Porthos   Aramis
♠ Q J 6 2   ♠ 5 4 3
♡ J 10 7 5   ♡ 6 3
◊ 8 6   ◊ K Q J 7 5
♣ 8 7 5   ♣ K 6 4

                        Athos
                        ♠ A K 10 7
                        ♡ K 9 4 2
                        ◊ A 10 3
                        ♣ J 2

The bidding: South   North

                            1 ♠   2 ♣
                            2 NT   3 NT

Aramis led the ♡ 3, but had to take it up again, and as Athos did not want any penalty Porthos was allowed to play any card he liked. Porthos decided to lead the ◇ 8. Thus Aramis' diamonds were established before dummy's clubs, and Athos went one down. When Athos asked Porthos where he got the idea to lead a diamond Porthos replied:

'Well, I didn't think it fair to lead the suit that Aramis had shown, and both the black suits having been bid there were only diamonds left!'

South/N–S.

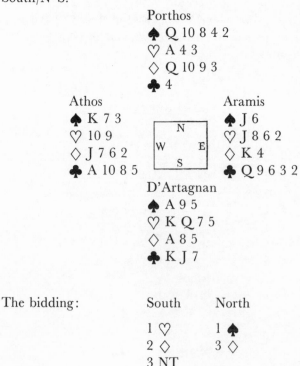

                          Porthos
                          ♠ Q 10 8 4 2
                          ♡ A 4 3
                          ◇ Q 10 9 3
                          ♣ 4
      Athos   Aramis
      ♠ K 7 3   ♠ J 6
      ♡ 10 9   ♡ J 8 6 2
      ◇ J 7 6 2   ◇ K 4
      ♣ A 10 8 5   ♣ Q 9 6 3 2
                          D'Artagnan
                          ♠ A 9 5
                          ♡ K Q 7 5
                          ◇ A 8 5
                          ♣ K J 7

The bidding: South   North

                            1 ♡   1 ♠
                            2 ◇   3 ◇
                            3 NT

Athos led his lowest club, and d'Artagnan took Aramis' ♣ 9 with the ♣ J. He cashed the ♠ A and continued with the ♠ 9, but before Athos had even touched the ♠ 7 which he was intending to play, Aramis was holding the ♡ 2 in such a way that d'Artagnan could not help seeing it. It will never be known whether the ever suspicious d'Artagnan smelled a rat or whether he would have let the ♠ 9 ride. Athos, who would never cheat, preferred to go up with the king and Aramis, crestfallen, had to play the jack. Athos continued with the ♣ 8. D'Artagnan won with the ♣ K and cashed three high spades and three high hearts. Athos then discarded the ♣ A and the ♣ 10 to guard diamonds, and Aramis threw the ◊ 4. The result was that d'Artagnan won twelve tricks which, in Aramis' opinion, was the double of what he should have scored without Athos' gentlemanly behaviour.

East/Both.

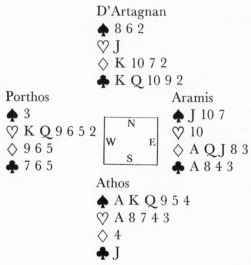

D'Artagnan
♠ 8 6 2
♡ J
◊ K 10 7 2
♣ K Q 10 9 2

Porthos
♠ 3
♡ K Q 9 6 5 2
◊ 9 6 5
♣ 7 6 5

Aramis
♠ J 10 7
♡ 10
◊ A Q J 8 3
♣ A 8 4 3

Athos
♠ A K Q 9 5 4
♡ A 8 7 4 3
◊ 4
♣ J

The bidding:

East	South	West	North
1 ◇	Pass!	1 ♡	Pass
2 ◇	2 ♠	Pass	3 ♠
Pass	4 ♠		

When 1 ◇ was bid Athos preferred to pass and postpone his bidding until later. Porthos led the ◇ 9 which was covered by the ◇ 10 and taken by Aramis with the ◇ J. He shifted to the ♡ 10. Athos was well aware that Aramis would not play a heart if he could not overruff dummy, and therefore must be holding a singleton. So he went up with the ace and drew three rounds of trumps. Then he took the ♣ J over with dummy's ♣ Q. Aramis might just as well take it at once and so he shifted to the ◇ A. But as everyone is aware Athos was always willing to give his opponents some small gift—and he threw a low heart. Aramis now had to play a diamond or a club to dummy, and Athos was able to get rid of all his heart losers.

The error that Porthos made on the next deal was due neither to stupidity nor to skill, but only to not paying attention. But it led to a surprising result.

South/Both.

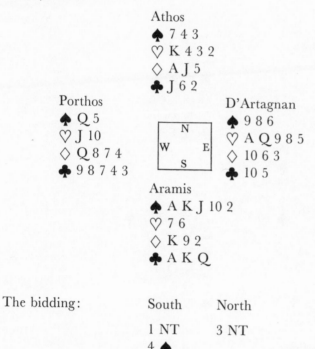

Athos
♠ 7 4 3
♡ K 4 3 2
◇ A J 5
♣ J 6 2

Porthos
♠ Q 5
♡ J 10
◇ Q 8 7 4
♣ 9 8 7 4 3

D'Artagnan
♠ 9 8 6
♡ A Q 9 8 5
◇ 10 6 3
♣ 10 5

Aramis
♠ A K J 10 2
♡ 7 6
◇ K 9 2
♣ A K Q

The bidding:

South	North
1 NT	3 NT
4 ♠	

Porthos opened with the ♡ J. Aramis covered with dummy's king and d'Artagnan took it with the ace, continuing with the ♡ Q and the ♡ 8. Aramis ruffed with the ♠ 10 and Porthos discarded the ♣ 3! The trump queen thus being unveiled in East Aramis refrained from finessing in diamonds so as not to risk another heart lead. He played the ◇ 2 to the ace to take the 'certain' trump finesse with the ♠ J; but Porthos took the trick with the ♠ Q, and asked:

'What exactly are we playing?'

When he was told that the contract was 4 ♠ he protested and said that he thought that it was 3 No Trumps. And if it was not he could have taken the trick long ago. So Porthos exited in clubs and later got a diamond trick, thus setting the contract. If he had overruffed in the third trick Aramis would, of course, have finessed in diamonds and made the contract.

South/Both.

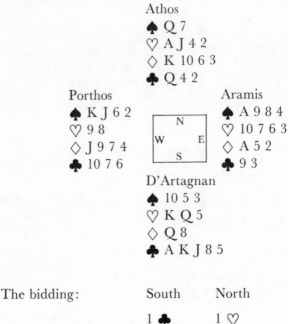

Athos
♠ Q 7
♡ A J 4 2
◇ K 10 6 3
♣ Q 4 2

Porthos
♠ K J 6 2
♡ 9 8
◇ J 9 7 4
♣ 10 7 6

Aramis
♠ A 9 8 4
♡ 10 7 6 3
◇ A 5 2
♣ 9 3

D'Artagnan
♠ 10 5 3
♡ K Q 5
◇ Q 8
♣ A K J 8 5

The bidding:

South	North
1 ♣	1 ♡
1 NT	3 NT

Porthos led his lowest diamond, and Aramis went up with the ace. Seeing no future in diamonds he shifted to the ♠ 4. D'Artagnan saw that by ordinary means he would be beaten. But his imagination saw the way of counter-attacking. When Porthos won the trick with the ♠ K d'Artagnan 'unblocked' the ♠ Q from dummy! Porthos could only see that the reason for this was that d'Artagnan held the ♠ A–10 and would try to create two entries if he, Porthos, continued in spades. This favour he would not grant and so he shifted to hearts. D'Artagnan took the rest: Eleven tricks.

East/Both.

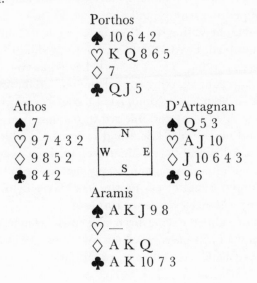

Porthos
♠ 10 6 4 2
♡ K Q 8 6 5
◇ 7
♣ Q J 5

Athos
♠ 7
♡ 9 7 4 3 2
◇ 9 8 5 2
♣ 8 4 2

D'Artagnan
♠ Q 5 3
♡ A J 10
◇ J 10 6 4 3
♣ 9 6

Aramis
♠ A K J 9 8
♡ —
◇ A K Q
♣ A K 10 7 3

The bidding:

East	South	West	North
Pass	2 ♠	Pass	3 ♡
Pass	4 ♣	Pass	5 ♠
Pass	7 ♠	Pass	Pass
Dble.	Redble.		

In accordance with the lead-directing double Athos led the
♡ 3. D'Artagnan covered dummy's queen with the ace. This,
however, was ruffed by Aramis, who glanced suspiciously at
d'Artagnan. The latter's face was expressionless and Aramis
could not expect that d'Artagnan would give any hint if he,
in fact, held three spades to the queen. So he took it for
granted, therefore, that the double was intended only to be
lead-directing, and he drew two rounds of spades from the
top. And now d'Artagnan could allow himself a smile.

Aramis exlaimed crossly:

'Really, d'Artagnan, I would never have believed it of you

to make such a bad double. In any case, you know. I would
have topped the trumps and gone one down.'

'You may be saying so,' d'Artagnan replied, 'but even if I
hadn't doubled, hearts would without any doubt have been
led. Are you trying to lead me to believe that you would not
have put on your thinking-cap when you had found me with
the ♡ A without having doubled? Of course, you would have
at once smelled a rat and finessed in trumps. And then how
you would have smiled! So I had to try the double-cross!'

At first Athos and Porthos had been inclined to agree with
Aramis, but after d'Artagnan's reply they knew full well that
it was simply a matter of one ruthless player being double-
crossed by another even more ruthless.

The last rubber having been played d'Artagnan tried to
delay the moment of leave-taking by telling about a deal he
had played with some chance acquaintances:

East/Love all.

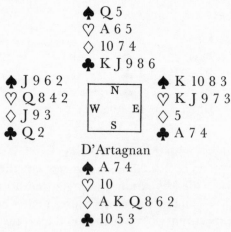

```
                    ♠ Q 5
                    ♡ A 6 5
                    ◇ 10 7 4
                    ♣ K J 9 8 6
  ♠ J 9 6 2                        ♠ K 10 8 3
  ♡ Q 8 4 2         N              ♡ K J 9 7 3
  ◇ J 9 3       W       E          ◇ 5
  ♣ Q 2             S              ♣ A 7 4
                    D'Artagnan
                    ♠ A 7 4
                    ♡ 10
                    ◇ A K Q 8 6 2
                    ♣ 10 5 3
```

The bidding:

East	South	West	North
1 ♡	2 ◇	2 ♡	2 NT
Pass	4 ◇	Pass	5 ◇

West had led the ♡ 2 which d'Artagnan had taken with dummy's ace, and then drawn three rounds of trumps. He then played the ♣ 10 which no one would take. The ♣ Q came from West on the next round and was covered with the ♣ K, but East wisely ducked again. Now it was no idea to establish the clubs without an entry, but as East had dropped two hearts on the trumps d'Artagnan ruffed a heart and exited in clubs to East's ace. East tried to exit with the ♡ K, but d'Artagnan let him hold it. And so East had to lead away from the ♠ K—and d'Artagnan made the contract.

Aramis then sketched a plan which corresponded exactly with that which d'Artagnan had played.

'Yes,' d'Artagnan agreed, 'you would, of course, have made the contract if you had been sitting in my place, but not if I had been sitting where East was. Look, I will discard a couple of spades instead of hearts, and then when you endplay me on the ♣ A I could go on playing hearts until doomsday.'

Athos then started to play in the same way, but after having had to abandon clubs and ruffed a heart he drew all the trumps and the following end-position was reached:

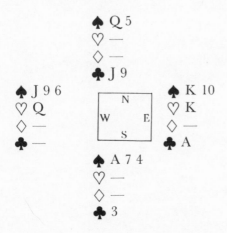

'You see,' Athos said, 'East is squeezed. He is endplayed on the ♣ A and can only cash the ♡ K, and so must lead away from the ♠ K.'

'Agreed,' d'Artagnan answered, 'but not with me in East for the simple reason that I have the ♡ 7 left and not the blank ♡ K.'

Porthos came into the argument here by saying:

'I cannot follow you in all your endplays and squeezes. After I have taken the first trick with the ♡ A I will play the ♠ 5 to the ace and another spade. I can ruff the third spade and will later lose only a club trick. Too easy!'

TEN YEARS AFTER

Another ten years have rolled by. The four friends were never to meet again, but on one occasion three of them did for a short time.

Louis XIV was not yet known as the 'Sun King'. D'Artagnan had retired from the army and one day visited Planchet in his shop in the rue des Lombards to tell him of his scheme, and its carrying out, to capture General Monk over in England. Planchet invested the money for the adventure, which succeeded beyond all expectations. When Charles II returned to the throne d'Artagnan found himself a wealthy man. He repaid Planchet, who advised him to invest part of his capital in a house on the Place de Grève which would give him a good income from rentals, and partly in another property—an inn called 'L'Image de Notre-Dame', the windows on the first floor being available for hiring out when executions took place in front of the inn. These transactions were duly celebrated with a number of bottles of wine. From memory d'Artagnan told Planchet of a number of deals which he might care to add to his collection. In fact some of them were played in this same inn about thirty years previously.

South/Both.

D'Artagnan
♠ A 10 9 5 2
♡ 4 3 2
◇ J 6
♣ A 5 2

Porthos   Aramis
♠ J 8 7 6 3   ♠ K
♡ K Q 8 6   ♡ J 5
◇ 4   ◇ Q 9 8 7 2
♣ J 8 6   ♣ Q 9 7 4 3

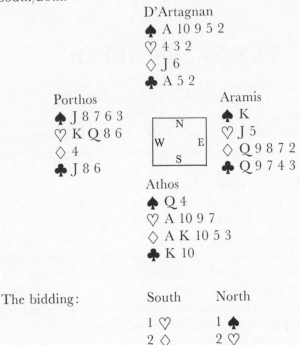

Athos
♠ Q 4
♡ A 10 9 7
◇ A K 10 5 3
♣ K 10

The bidding: South   North

                    1 ♡   1 ♠
                    2 ◇   2 ♡
                    2 NT   3 NT

Porthos opened with the ♣ 6, the only unbid suit, and
Athos took the queen with the king. He played the ♠ Q,
letting it ride to Aramis' blank king, and the next trick
Porthos was allowed to hold with the ♣ J. Porthos continued
with the ♣ 8 to dummy's ace. Athos throwing the ♡ 10. At
this particular point in the play Athos could not overlook the
eventual importance of this discard; he was aware, nevertheless, that if he should play on the spades he would need
several discards, and it would then not matter if he threw the
♡ 7 later. Quite the contrary—it might confuse his opponents.

Athos then played the ◇ J from dummy. Aramis covered
with the ◇ Q, which was in turn taken by the ace. Hoping
for a lucky diamond distribution Athos cashed the ◇ K.
Porthos threw the ♠ 6 which did not please Athos, for it

meant that Porthos still held that suit sufficiently guarded, or that Aramis held the ♠ J. To give Porthos the 'opportunity' of another discard Athos cashed the ◇ 10, and if Porthos' subconscious mind had now worked as did that of Athos earlier he would have thrown the ♡ 8. Instead he discarded the ♡ 6. Athos played the ♠ 4, finessing with the ♠ 9 which unveiled the distribution of the spades. He did not give up but played the ♡ 4 and finessed with the ♡ 9. Porthos took the trick with the ♡ Q, but finally realising what was going on, in desperation he played the ♡ K. But Athos won with the ♡ A and put Porthos into lead again on the ♡ 8, following which Porthos had to lead spades into dummy's tenace.

South/N–S.

Athos
♠ A 8 6 5
♡ K 9 6 4
◇ 10 6
♣ 8 6 5

Aramis
♠ K Q J 10 4
♡ 10 8 3
◇ 8 5 2
♣ J 10

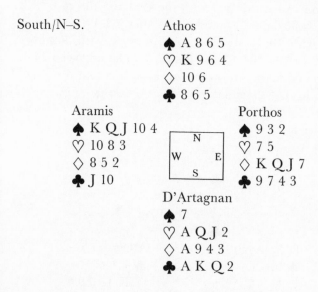

Porthos
♠ 9 3 2
♡ 7 5
◇ K Q J 7
♣ 9 7 4 3

D'Artagnan
♠ 7
♡ A Q J 2
◇ A 9 4 3
♣ A K Q 2

The bidding:

South	West	North	East
1 ♡	1 ♠	2 ♡	Pass
2 ♠	Pass	3 ♠	Pass
4 NT	Pass	5 ◇	Pass
6 ♡			

Aramis led the ♠ K which was taken with dummy's ace. D'Artagnan did not need very long to count the tricks that could be made. As there were hardly more than three club tricks and one diamond trick he would therefore need seven trump tricks. But as dummy's trumps were not big enough, and the entries so few, he had instead to play for six trump tricks and an extra trick in one of the minors. In those days there were no books on 'How to play bridge', and such things as 'squeeze', 'dummy reversal' and 'unnecessary finesse' d'Artagnan had to invent—and this he did!

On the second trick he ruffed the ♠ 5 with the ♡ J! He then cashed the ◊ A and continued with the ◊ 3. Porthos won and shifted to the ♣ 3 which was taken by the ace. Then d'Artagnan ruffed the ◊ 4 with the ♡ 4 and the ♠ 6 with the ♡ Q, cashed the ♡ A and played the ♡ 2. When Aramis followed with the ♡ 8, d'Artagnan finessed with dummy's ♡ 9 and cashed the ♡ K. Porthos could not keep both diamonds and clubs, and when he threw a club d'Artagnan discarded his last diamond and took the rest in clubs.

South/Love all.

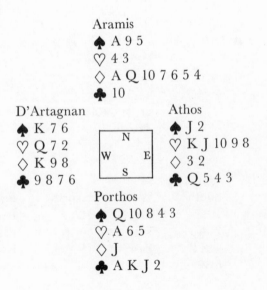

Aramis
♠ A 9 5
♡ 4 3
◊ A Q 10 7 6 5 4
♣ 10

D'Artagnan
♠ K 7 6
♡ Q 7 2
◊ K 9 8
♣ 9 8 7 6

Athos
♠ J 2
♡ K J 10 9 8
◊ 3 2
♣ Q 5 4 3

Porthos
♠ Q 10 8 4 3
♡ A 6 5
◊ J
♣ A K J 2

South/Love all.

              Athos
              ♠ 6 3
              ♡ J 6
              ◇ 5 3
              ♣ A Q J 9 7 5 3

Aramis   D'Artagnan
♠ K J 9 8   ♠ 7 5 2
♡ K 5 2   N   ♡ A 9 8 3
◇ 10 4 2   W   E   ◇ K J 9 7 6
♣ K 8 6   S   ♣ 4

              Baisemeaux
              ♠ A Q 10 4
              ♡ Q 10 7 4
              ◇ A Q 8
              ♣ 10 2

The bidding:

	South	North
	1 ♠	2 ♣
	2 ♡	3 ♣
	3 NT	

Aramis led the ◇ 10 which Baisemeaux took with the queen, then to play the ♣ 10 and let it ride. At the very moment when Baisemeaux touched dummy's ♣ 3 Aramis reached out his hand as if to scrape the trick home—but the ♣ 10 held the trick. Baisemeaux fell into the trap and thought that d'Artagnan held up the ♣ K. Since, however, Aramis followed to the next club with the ♣ 8 the king had to be blank. So Baisemeaux went up with the ♣ A—and five nice club tricks had gone to waste.

The bidding:

	South	North
	1 ♠	2 ◇
	3 ♣	4 ♠
	6 ♠	

With the object of compelling Porthos to take an immediate stand to an eventual diamond finesse d'Artagnan led the ◇ 9. Porthos had the feeling that this was a singleton, so he went up with the ace, and then played the ♣ 10, letting it ride and it held. He then played the ♡ 4 to the ace, cashed the ♣ A–K to throw a heart and a diamond from dummy and cross-ruffed hearts and diamonds until the following position was reached:

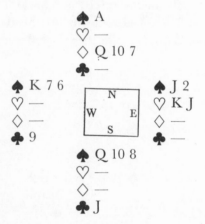

Now Porthos ruffed the ♣ J with dummy's ♠ A and played the ◇ Q, ruffing with the ♠ 10 when Athos threw the ♡ J. If d'Artagnan had overruffed, Porthos would have taken the rest — but d'Artagnan underruffed with the ♠ 6! As a result Porthos had to lead away from the ♠ Q–8, and thus gave his opponents the last two tricks.

As is known, the young King Louis XIV had every intention of assuming absolute power on Cardinal Mazarin's death. The King wished d'Artagnan, now a Captain in the Musketeers, to resume duty in his service and made him an offer which could not be resisted. At this time Athos had come to Paris to speak to the King about his son's marriage, but the King himself was interested in this particular young lady, and in the event, Athos so offended Louis that d'Artagnan was ordered by him to arrest Athos. D'Artagnan carried out his instruction with the idea in his mind that by so doing he could help Athos to escape. But Athos refused all suggestions made to him and demanded to be arrested. So he was taken to the Bastille where he was met by Governor Baisemeaux. Quite by chance Aramis happened at that pariruclar time to be seeing Baisemeaux on a business matter.

Saying nothing to Aramis and Baisemeaux about the arrest d'Artagnan left Athos in their company while he reported back to the King who finally agreed to cancel the warrant for Athos' arrest. And when he returned to the Bastille it was Baisemeaux who requested the three old friends to have a hand of bridge with him.

East/Love all.

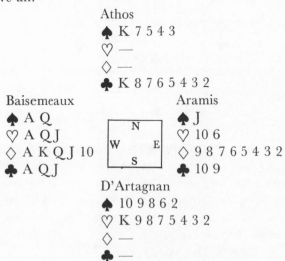

Athos
♠ K 7 5 4 3
♡ —
◇ —
♣ K 8 7 6 5 4 3 2

Baisemeaux
♠ A Q
♡ A Q J
◇ A K Q J 10
♣ A Q J

Aramis
♠ J
♡ 10 6
◇ 9 8 7 6 5 4 3 2
♣ 10 9

D'Artagnan
♠ 10 9 8 6 2
♡ K 9 8 7 5 4 3 2
◇ —
♣ —

The bidding:

East	South	West	North
Pass	4 ♡	4 NT	Pass
5 ◇	5 ♡	6 ◇	Pass
Pass	6 ♠	Dble.	Redble.

D'Artagnan was a very brave man when he bid the spad for the first time on the six-level, but when Baisemea doubled, and Athos redoubled, d'Artagnan knew that he ha done the correct thing. Notwithstanding the Governor's ow amazingly good hand the contract was ice-cold. Baisemeau opened with the ◇ K which d'Artagnan ruffed in dummy. He then played the ♣ 2 and ruffed in order to play the ♠ 6 from the closed hand. Baisemeaux went up with the ace and continued in diamonds, then ruffed with dummy's ♠ 5. After another club ruff with the ♠ 8, the ♠ 9 was played to the king, drawing the Governor's queen. A club was ruffed with the ♠ 10, and with the ♠ 7 as an entry all dummy's cards were high.

Who would have imagined that a 'sacrifice' of 7 ◇ would have been better? Unfortunately this suit had been bid first by East, and with the opening lead in South the contract could not be made. But in West's hand the grand slam would be cold because North would already have been endplayed before the first lead!

North/Love all.

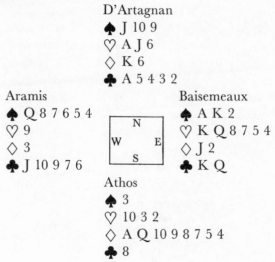

D'Artagnan
♠ J 10 9
♡ A J 6
◇ K 6
♣ A 5 4 3 2

Aramis
♠ Q 8 7 6 5 4
♡ 9
◇ 3
♣ J 10 9 7 6

Baisemeaux
♠ A K 2
♡ K Q 8 7 5 4
◇ J 2
♣ K Q

Athos
♠ 3
♡ 10 3 2
◇ A Q 10 9 8 7 5 4
♣ 8

The bidding:

North	East	South	West
1 ♣	Dble.	1 ◇	1 ♠
Pass	3 ♡	5 ◇	Pass
Pass	Dble.		

Aramis led his singleton ♡ 9. Athos played the ♡ 6 from dummy and the ♡ 3 from the closed hand. Baisemeaux, winning with the ♡ Q, could not see who held the ♡ 2 and would therefore not risk continuing in hearts, and all the more so as he apparently held two 'sure tricks' in spades which he hurried to cash—but Athos ruffed the second spade.

Athos now seized the opportunity to show that d'Artagnan was not the only one to achieve miracles at the card-table. He was d'Artagnan's equal as a player, but where it took d'Artagnan about five seconds to decide the run of play Athos needed rather more time.

It was clear that Aramis and Baisemeaux held the spade and heart stoppers respectively, and it was equally clear that a 'Vienne Coup' with a double squeeze was the solution. But there was the drawback that Athos could not draw all the trumps before cashing the ♡ A for the good reason that he could not then re-enter the closed hand without ruffing a squeeze card. So he had to suppose that Aramis held a singleton trump. Based on all these considerations Athos played a low trump to the ◇ K and cashed the ♡ A and, as he hoped, Aramis threw a spade. The rest was easy—trumps and trumps until the following situation was reached:

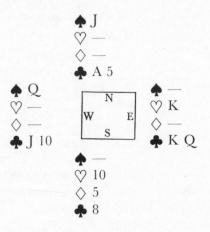

When Athos now cashed the ◇ 5 Aramis had to discard the ♣ 10. Dummy could then spare the ♠ J, but Baisemeaux could spare absolutely nothing—for he knew that Athos held the ♡ 10. He therefore discarded a club, and dummy took the last two tricks in clubs.

Baisemeaux was full of regret that he had not returned a heart to the second or third trick, but he was consoled by d'Artagnan who told him that he would not then have enjoyed the experience of seeing some very ingenious play.

EPILOGUE

Four years passed by. Porthos and Athos had died. Aramis was living in Spain where he had attained a dukedom. D'Artagnan was in the Sun King's highest favour. He had been entrusted with the command of the French Army in the campaign against Holland. Never had a campaign been better directed, and in the course of a single month twelve fortresses had been captured. While the siege of the thirteenth was proceeding a messenger arrived from the King and Colbert to hand over to d'Artagnan his marshal's baton. At the very moment he was receiving it a cannonball fired from the fortress hit him in the chest. He had just sufficient strength left to take the baton in his hand and direct a new attack. Indeed, he lived long enough to see the white flag of surrender being hoisted on this very thirteenth fortress.

It seemed as if he were smiling because of the new victory. In reality his thoughts during those last few minutes were with his three friends and the several times he had battled for the thirteenth trick—and surely this 'Coup de Grace' was among his fondest memories:

North/Both.

Athos
♠ A K Q 10 5
♡ K Q 6 2
◇ 7
♣ A 9 4

Porthos
♠ 9 7
♡ J 10 9
◇ 10 5 4 3 2
♣ K 8 5

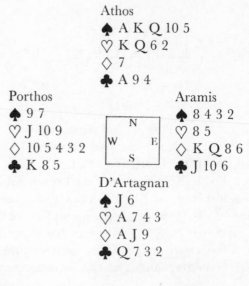

Aramis
♠ 8 4 3 2
♡ 8 5
◇ K Q 8 6
♣ J 10 6

D'Artagnan
♠ J 6
♡ A 7 4 3
◇ A J 9
♣ Q 7 3 2

The bidding:

	North	South
	1 ♠	2 ♡
	4 NT	5 ♡
	7 ♡	

Porthos led the ♡ J. D'Artagnan won and continued with two more rounds of trumps and five rounds of spades. Aramis discarded a diamond and a club, and d'Artagnan threw three low clubs from the closed hand. Then a diamond to the ace led to the following situation:

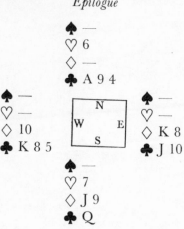

Now came the 'Coup de Grace'—the ♣ Q from the closed hand. Porthos had to cover with the king. Dummy won with the ♣ A, the ♣ 4 was ruffed with the ♡ 7, and with the ♡ 6 as an entry on a diamond ruff the ♣ 9 was good for the last trick.

Thirteen fortresses—and all thirteen tricks!

When he wrote about d'Artagnan's death Planchet's descendant was not ashamed to admit that he had to wipe away a tear—just as he had to do every time he had finished reading the 'Musketeers' trilogy, and just as Alexandre Dumas himself had to do when the estimable Porthos was killed.